Mistress of Novices

A Play

John Kerr

A Samuel French Acting Edition

SAMUELFRENCH-LONDON.CO.UK
SAMUELFRENCH.COM

Copyright © 1973 by John Kerr
All Rights Reserved

MISTRESS OF NOVICES is fully protected under the copyright laws of the British Commonwealth, including Canada, the United States of America, and all other countries of the Copyright Union. All rights, including professional and amateur stage productions, recitation, lecturing, public reading, motion picture, radio broadcasting, television and the rights of translation into foreign languages are strictly reserved.

ISBN 978-0-573-06012-0

www.samuelfrench-london.co.uk

www.samuelfrench.com

For Amateur Production Enquiries

United Kingdom and World
excluding north america
plays@SamuelFrench-London.co.uk
020 7255 4302/01

Each title is subject to availability from Samuel French,

depending upon country of performance.

CAUTION: Professional and amateur producers are hereby warned that *MISTRESS OF NOVICES* is subject to a licensing fee. Publication of this play does not imply availability for performance. Both amateurs and professionals considering a production are strongly advised to apply to the appropriate agent before starting rehearsals, advertising, or booking a theatre. A licensing fee must be paid whether the title is presented for charity or gain and whether or not admission is charged.

The professional rights in this play are controlled by Eric Glass Ltd, 25 Ladbroke Crescent, London, W11 1PS.

No one shall make any changes in this title for the purpose of production. No part of this book may be reproduced, stored in a retrieval system, or transmitted in any form, by any means, now known or yet to be invented, including mechanical, electronic, photocopying, recording, videotaping, or otherwise, without the prior written permission of the publisher. No one shall upload this title, or part of this title, to any social media websites.

The right of John Kerr to be identified as author of this work has been asserted by him in accordance with Section 77 of the Copyright, Designs and Patents Act 1988

MISTRESS OF NOVICES

First presented by Triarch Productions Ltd at the Opera House, Manchester, on 7th November 1972, subsequently transferring to the Piccadilly Theatre, London, on 15th February 1973, with the following cast of characters:

First Reader	Linda Gray
Second Reader	Hermione Gregory
Mother Josephine Imbert	Margaretta Scott
Sister Marthe Fores	Beau Daniels
Bishop of Nevers	Geoffrey Keen
Mother Marie-Therese Vauzou	Barbara Jefford
Sister Emilienne Duboe	Heather Bell
Sister Vincent Garros	Jill Raymond
Sister Bernard Dalias	Sally Reymond
Sister Stanislas Paschal	Valerie Verdon
Mother Alexandre Roque	Brenda Kempner
Bernadette Soubirous	Rita Tushingham
Father Douce	Joss Clewes
Doctor St Cyr	Brandon Brady
Sister Louise Cartier	Karen Ford
Two Nuns	Jean Ainslie
	Pat Brackenbury

The play directed by Charles Hickman

Setting by Berkeley Sutcliffe

ACT I
    Scene 1   Mother Josephine Imbert's Study, 1866
    Scene 2   The Great Hall of the Novitiate, 1866
    Scene 3   Mother Josephine Imbert's Study, 1866
    Scene 4   Bernadette's Room in the Infirmary, 1866
    Scene 5   The Great Hall of the Novitiate, 1867

ACT II
    Scene 1   The Infirmary, 1868
    Scene 2   Mother Josephine Imbert's Study, 1868
    Scene 3   The Chapel, 1878
    Scene 4   Bernadette's Room in the Infirmary, 1878
    Scene 5   A room in the Hospice of Mary Immaculate in Lourdes, 1906

AUTHOR'S NOTE

The Convent of Saint Gildard in Nevers was built in 1856. The action of the play begins in 1866, therefore the play is set in a comparatively new building. Like all houses of religion it has a stark simplicity. The furniture and adornments are minimal.

The linking scenes of the Readers reading from the Community Journal are to facilitate the smooth flow of the play; there should be no Black-Outs. As the lights dim at the end of a scene, they should immediately rise on the two Readers at opposite sides of the stage, while the main acting area is being changed.

The play may well be presented in soft tabs and wings. The original production was mounted on a false stage, and projected pictures of Nevers and Lourdes were shown before the start of the play and before Act II, Scene 5, respectively.

COSTUME PLOT

All **Fully Professed Nuns** wear a black habit and veil. They wear a white wimple with starched tabs under their chins, and starched white collars covering their shoulders. They do not wear a crucifix nor a wedding-ring in this order.

In Act I, Scene 4, **Sister Marthe Fores** wears a large white apron. In Act II, Scene 1, **Sister Marthe Fores, Sister Vincent Garros** and **Sister Emilienne Duboe** all wear white aprons—which they also wear in Act II, Scene 4.

The **Postulants** wear long black full-skirted dresses with black shoulder capes. They wear small black bonnets tied under their chins at all times. As **Novices** they wear white veils with their full nuns' costumes.

Bernadette, on her first entrance, wears a long peasant dress of blue and white checked cotton, a denim blue apron, a grey shawl, and a yellow and red headscarf. In bed she wears a white woollen nightdress with long sleeves, and a white bonnet.

The **Bishop** wears a black bishop's cassock piped in red with a red skull-cap in Act I, Scenes 1, 2, and 3—a red cloak is added to this costume in Scenes 2 and 3. He also wears the black cassock in Act II, Scene 5. In Act I, Scene 5, he wears a scarlet cassock.

The **Doctor** wears a brown tweed frock-coated suit in Act I—a similar suit in grey in Act II.

Father Douce wears a black cassock with black and white cravat tabs.

ACT I

Scene 1

The Lights come up on two Readers standing on either side of the stage

First Reader The Convent of St Gildard in Nevers.

During the reading, Nuns bring on the office furniture for the scene and silently file off.
    Mother Josephine and Mother Marie-Therese enter from opposite sides. They bow, and Mother Marie-Therese crosses and exits

Mother Josephine goes to the desk, picks up a letter, and sits

Sister Marthe enters

The Lights come up full as Mother Josephine signs the letter and gives it to Sister Marthe. There is a knock off stage

Sister Marthe takes the letter, exits, and returns with the Bishop

Mother Josephine rises to greet him, then sits at the desk. The Bishop sits

(*During the Above*) The Mother House of the Order of Sisters of Charity and Christian instruction.
Second Reader The Feast of St Peter and St Paul, June the twenty-ninth, eighteen hundred and sixty-six.

Sister Marthe exits

Bishop You know why I have come?
Josephine I know why you have come, your Lordship.
Bishop And your decision?
Josephine It has not altered.
Bishop They say her health has improved.
Josephine She is still a chronic asthmatic.
Bishop But her recuperative powers are said to be remarkable.
Josephine A house of religion is no place for an invalid.
Bishop Even if the invalid should be the visionary of Lourdes?
Josephine I have a duty toward my community.
Bishop Your community would be graced by her admittance.
Josephine Some other community should be so graced. Our Order is a practical one.
Bishop With a supernatural vocation, Mother Josephine.

Josephine The girl is neither qualified to nurse nor to teach.
Bishop Her initial period here in the Mother House would enable her to learn a profession.
Josephine But I am told that she's barely literate!
Bishop Quite untrue, but you might have to fill a few gaps in her education.
Josephine Your Lordship, the girl would be useless here.
Bishop (*chuckling*) The Bishop of Tarbes says she has a remarkable facility for peeling vegetables.
Josephine This is no laughing matter, your Lordship. She is said to be retarded.
Bishop Physically.
Josephine And mentally.
Bishop Physically, Mother Josephine. Her education has suffered at the expense of her health.
Josephine I have said it repeatedly, and I say it again, she may join us when she is capable.
Bishop (*rising*) What of her future, then?
Josephine That decision is not mine, your Lordship.
Bishop That decision concerns us all.
Josephine She is well cared for by the sisters at Lourdes.
Bishop They can no longer control the cult created around her. At the consecration of the crypt last month, her clothes would have been torn from her body but for the intervention of the police.
Josephine A similar situation would be calamitous here.
Bishop Such a situation would never arise here. Her whereabouts would remain secret.
Josephine A secret from the world possibly. But within these four walls —never. Her intrusion would shatter the discipline necessary to the religious life.
Bishop Reverend Mother, there is no more suitable convent in the world for this girl.
Josephine There is no room in this house for a passenger.
Bishop Believe me, it is expedient that she comes here.
Josephine Without my consent?
Bishop Your consent is necessary. I would advise you to give it.
Josephine And if I refuse?
Bishop If you refuse you are likely to bring the wrath of officialdom upon your head. Already Rome is querying her delay in entering the religious life.
Josephine Surely you have explained my point of view?
Bishop (*wearily*) Mother Josephine, her admittance to this house is inevitable. Of this you are well aware. So why delay your consent?

After a pause, Mother Josephine rings a handbell

Sister Marthe enters

Josephine Please summon the Mistress of Novices.

Sister Marthe exits

Bishop Your position is not without compensation. Mother Josephine.
Josephine (*rising*) I am blinded by the impracticality of my position.
Bishop Every other convent in France has courted her!
Josephine How unfortunate that she was not persuaded to accept the hand of a contemplative order.
Bishop On the surface a contemplative order does appear to be more appropriate. But she could not withstand the physical rigours.
Josephine We have never made special dispensation to any of our novices.
Bishop She doesn't ask for any. She has chosen a rule she feels she can follow.
Josephine (*after a pause*) Is a religious life imperative?
Bishop Your naïveté surprises me, Reverend Mother.
Josephine It is equally naïve to assume that supernatural experiences are proof of a vocation.
Bishop She believes her vocation to be true.
Josephine And so do many young women, until they are put to the test.
Bishop Would you deny her that privilege?
Josephine I deny her nothing. But once within these walls, she will not be privileged because of her background.

There is a tap at the door and Mother Marie-Therese Vauzou, Mistress of Novices, enters. She is a woman of strong personality, overbearing almost, in her early forties

Mother Marie-Therese, I have reluctantly agreed that Mademoiselle Soubirous should join the community.
Marie-Therese (*ecstatically*) Our prayers have been answered.
Josephine Your prayers may have been answered, Mother.
Marie-Therese What a grace it will be to receive this privileged child. We are most grateful, your Lordship.
Bishop Some appear to be more grateful than others, Mother.
Marie-Therese It will be the greatest blessing of my life to behold the eyes that have seen the Blessed Virgin herself!
Josephine (*impatiently*) Yes, yes. Contain your exuberance for a while. There are matters to be discussed.
Marie-Therese First, the dowry.
Josephine There is a customary dowry agreed upon by the community...
Bishop (*interrupting*) The child is impoverished.
Josephine Nobody is so impoverished that they can't provide the pittance required by our Order.
Bishop Some are blessed with earthly riches, others are more enriched spiritually. In this case there is no dowry.
Marie-Therese A dowry is essential for a bride of God!
Bishop There have been exceptions.
Josephine Only when the candidates were able-bodied, and offered compensation by the strength of their vocations.

Bishop Who can judge the strength of a vocation until it is put to the test?
Marie-Therese I could arrange private donation for the dowry.
Josephine That will not be necessary. The dowry shall be donated by the community.
Marie-Therese And her clothing?
Josephine I donate sixty francs for her clothing.
Bishop Thank you, Mother Josephine.
Josephine Finance is a mere formality, your Lordship.
Bishop And having disposed of it, what of the principal matter?
Josephine Her actual moulding to the religious life?
Bishop Yes.
Josephine As Mistress of Novices, Mother Marie-Therese is highly respected for her spiritual guidance.
Bishop This is an exceptional case.
Josephine Among the novitiate there are no exceptional cases. They are all on the common road.
Bishop Is there nothing exceptional about a girl who is being proclaimed a saint by the people in her own lifetime?
Marie-Therese She will receive no adulation here.
Bishop Nor would she desire it. She has a tendency to shyness, and she finds the lack of privacy in Lourdes repugnant. She wishes only to disappear from the world.
Josephine She may have become accustomed to adulation, all the same. What will happen when she finds herself suddenly deprived of it?
Bishop What do you fear?
Josephine The effect she may have on my sisters.
Bishop The sisters should be secure in their vocations.
Josephine And how will their curiosity affect her? In the confines of a religious house she will be more vulnerable to attention, and the consequent danger of an inflated ego.
Marie-Therese There is nothing to fear. I will protect her from her own pride.
Josephine You make it sound like a simple theological exercise.
Marie-Therese Theoretically, it is.
Bishop But in practice we are dealing with a human being. I hope you are not underestimating the responsibility which is being placed upon your shoulders.
Marie-Therese Are you doubting my ability, your Lordship?
Bishop Not at all, Mother. I am merely trying to point out that this is a very individual case. A soul of extreme sensitivity and tenderness. How tragic if we were to misguide it.
Marie-Therese Never fear, your Lordship. We are well instructed in such matters. St John of the Cross deals with the treatment of visionaries at some length.
Bishop Are you aware of this, Mother Josephine?
Josephine Superficially, your Lordship.
Marie-Therese As the subject is within my particular domain I pursued it with more enthusiasm.
Bishop And your conclusions?

Act I, Scene 1 5

Marie-Therese In such people there is always an inherent danger to their humility. For her own good the girl's pride must be subjugated at all times.
Bishop And how do you propose to do that?
Josephine The question is premature, your Lordship. Mother Marie-Therese and I shall consider the subject and advise you accordingly.
Marie-Therese Oh, but I have already considered, Reverend Mother. I have indeed.
Bishop Even before her acceptance?
Marie-Therese I knew that it was God's will.
Bishop You have prophetic powers denied to us.
Marie-Therese I have denied myself sleep to pray that this chosen child would be entrusted to my care. And now that my prayers have been answered I am prepared with a suitable course of action.
Josephine Without my knowledge?
Marie-Therese As Mistress of Novices I shall be responsible for her spiritual guidance.
Josephine And as Mother-General I am responsible for the welfare of the whole community. You have overreached yourself, Mother.
Marie-Therese I stand rebuked, Reverend Mother. May I outline my plan, your Lordship?
Bishop Mother Josephine?
Josephine We are listening.
Marie-Therese From the start nobody in this house shall refer or enquire about the apparitions. Severest disciplinary action will be taken against any offenders.
Josephine I agree. Once her presence here is known there could be a complete collapse of discipline.
Marie-Therese Not if proper control is maintained. I intend to curb their curiosity by removing all mystery.
Bishop How?
Marie-Therese On her arrival she will address the entire community.
Josephine Mother Marie-Therese!
Marie-Therese She will tell her story, and answer any questions put to her.
Josephine But surely this is a blatant invitation to self-glory!
Marie-Therese Having satisfied their curiosity, there will be a complete silence. The subject will never be mentioned within these walls again.
Josephine (*sceptically*) To face the entire community is a little daunting at the best of times . . .
Bishop To someone with a tendency to shyness it would be unthinkable.
Marie-Therese Your Lordship, I consider it the only way.
Bishop Perhaps she could wait until she has become accustomed to the community?
Marie-Therese By then the mischief will have been done. I have decided that before she retreats into anonymity as many ears as possible shall hear her story.
Bishop The community is large.
Marie-Therese The sisters from the other orders in Nevers should benefit from this unique occasion.

Josephine Impossible! Our own community perhaps . . .
Marie-Therese I have already discussed it with all the relevant Mothers Superior.
Josephine (*outraged*) You had no right!
Marie-Therese I had every right.
Josephine I am still Mother-General!
Marie-Therese And I am your deputy during your periodic bouts of ill health. It was on one of these occasions that I considered it advisable to discuss the matter.
Josephine That will be all, Mother.
Marie-Therese When does she arrive, your Lordship?
Josephine I said that will be all!

Mother Marie-Therese takes her leave of the Bishop and departs

Bishop (*looking after her*) A very diligent woman, Mother Josephine.
Josephine A very trying one, your Lordship.
Bishop Enough to try the patience of the saints themselves.
Josephine Then I am obviously not destined for sanctity.
Bishop All the same. I think the girl will be safe in those strong hands. Not precluding your invaluable guidance, of course. How soon can you receive her, Reverend Mother?
Josephine We are waiting, your Lordship. I shall notify Lourdes immediately.
Bishop Thank you, Reverend Mother.

The Bishop and Reverend Mother exit

The Lights cross-fade to the two Readers

During the reading, the Nuns enter and clear the office furniture

LINKING SCENE

First Reader Entrance Book. July eight, eighteen hundred and sixty-six. Mademoiselle Bernadette Soubirous, postulant from Lourdes, aged twenty-two years.
Second Reader The Community Journal, July eighth, Mother Alexandre Roque, Principal of the Hospice of Lourdes, arrived at ten-thirty last night, accompanying Bernadette Soubirous. How happy we are to welcome her.
First Reader There had been much speculation amongst the community regarding Mademoiselle Soubirous's appearance. There is little to distinguish her from the other postulants, except perhaps for a more timid and retiring nature.

The Lights cross-fade to the Great Hall

Scene 2

The Great Hall of the Novitiate

The hall is bare. A lectern surmounted by a crucifix stands before the back wall

Mother Josephine and Mother Marie-Therese enter from one side of the stage, followed by four postulants. They are the future sisters Emilienne Duboe, Vincent Garros, Bernard Dalias, and Paschal. Simultaneously Mother Alexandre Roque enters from the opposite side with Bernadette Soubirous. The postulants form a line down one side of the stage. Mother Alexandre indicates for Bernadette to join them

Bernadette is pale and unsure of herself. She is drawn and tired from ill health. She gazes around the hall with awe, in direct contrast to the other postulants who stand with eyes piously downcast. She wears a check blue dress, a shawl, and her head is bound with a scarf. The other postulants are already clothed in black, with the small bonnets of the order

Josephine She looks pale.
Marie-Therese Her eyes are red.
Alexandre She cried herself to sleep last night.
Josephine Is she not happy to be here?
Alexandre To be here is her dearest wish.
Marie-Therese (*affectionately*) Tears are good for a vocation. They make it grow.
Josephine Thank you for that profound statement, Mother. It is quite untrue.

Josephine beckons Bernadette over

My daughter, we require a public duty of you.
Bernadette (*unsuspecting*) Whatever you wish, Reverend Mother!
Marie-Therese You will honour us with your story.
Bernadette (*uncomprehending*) Story?
Josephine Of the happenings at the grotto.

Bernadette recoils with shocked disbelief

Do you object?
Bernadette I came here to hide!
Josephine You came here to follow your vocation.
Bernadette How can I follow my vocation when it is continually being interrupted? For eight years I have been prodded and stared at like a caged animal.
Josephine Soon you will profess your vows of obedience. I suggest you start practising them now.

Bernadette humbly nods agreement

Sister Marthe, please see that the other sisters are all here.

Sister Marthe Fores leaves

There is a gentle hum of voices as the community supposedly files into the auditorium

Bernadette (*alarmed*) The sisters, Reverend Mother?
Josephine You will address the entire community before the bell of the midday Angelus.
Bernadette (*panic-stricken*) No . . .
Josephine Do you refuse my first request?
Bernadette No, Reverend Mother. (*Breathlessly*) I meant that I am nervous, I cannot face them . . .
Josephine Of course you can. They will want to hear what happened in Lourdes.
Bernadette But haven't they already heard?
Marie-Therese That supposition betrays an inclination to self-love. I shall record it as such.
Bernadette I meant—I have told it so many times before.
Marie-Therese Do you have an aversion to retelling so divine a privilege?
Bernadette Mother, what do you do with a broom?
Marie-Therese (*taken aback*) A broom! Why—sweep with it, I suppose.
Bernadette And then?
Marie-Therese One generally puts it back in its place. Why?
Bernadette And so with me. I have been used, and now I am happy to be put back in my place. I would be grateful to remain there, Mother.
Josephine Well spoken, my child. Record that as an inclination to modesty, Mother Marie-Therese.

Sister Marthe Fores returns

Are the sisters in their places?
Marthe Fores They are ready, Reverend Mother.

Mother Josephine addresses the audience as though they were her congregation of nuns

Josephine My Sisters, I welcome the new postulants to the community. You are all aware that Bernadette Soubirous, of Lourdes, has joined us today. To suppress any future curiosity, she will tell you of various supernatural experiences purported to have happened to her. When she has finished you will be free to ask questions. After that, there will be a complete and utter silence concerning the subject. It will never be mentioned within the walls of this house ever again. Do you understand?
Postulants Yes, Reverend Mother.
Josephine Bernadette Soubirous.

Bernadette looks around nervously

Come forward, my child, where everyone can see you.

Act I, Scene 2

Bernadette (*breathlessly*) Eight years ago, together with my sister Toinette and a friend, I went to gather firewood. We crossed the meadows to the cliff of Massabielle. The two other girls waded through the stream to the foot of the cliff. I was afraid to enter because I suffer from asthma. They ran off and left me. (*She pauses at the first sign of an asthmatic wheeze*) I sat down and started to remove my shoes and stockings, when I heard a sound like wind blowing through the trees. I looked around, but everything was still. Then my eyes were drawn toward the grotto. (*She pauses again*)
Josephine And what did you see?
Bernadette I saw a lady dressed in white, with a blue sash, and a golden rose on each foot. I was frightened. I rubbed my eyes because I could not believe what I was seeing. I reached for my rosary, and tried to make the sign of the cross. But my arms felt heavy and would not move. Then the lady herself made the sign of the cross. My hand began to tremble, and I could move it again. I said my rosary as the lady made the motions of saying hers. When I had finished she suddenly disappeared. (*She stops and looks enquiringly at Mother Josephine*)
Josephine Continue, my child.
Bernadette That's all, Reverend Mother.
Josephine She appeared to you more than once!
Bernadette Eighteen times in all.
Josephine Well, tell us.
Alexandre The waters, Bernadette. Tell us about the spring.
Bernadette During her ninth appearance the lady told me to drink at the spring and wash in it. I looked around the grotto, but couldn't find any water. So I started to walk back to the stream. (*She goes down on one knee*) The lady beckoned me back and indicated a place. I scratched in the dirt and found a little mud there. I touched my lips with it, and smeared it over my face.
Josephine This was one of the reasons you were accused of insanity, I believe?
Bernadette (*nodding*) They tried to have me locked up.
Josephine Please continue.
Bernadette But afterwards a trickle appeared out of the mud. And the trickle gushed into a spring.
Marie-Therese The lame are said to be healed after immersion in this water.
Bernadette (*rising*) So I'm told, Mother.
Marie-Therese As a tool of the discovery of this spring could it not be used to heal your own afflictions?
Bernadette The spring is not for me, Mother. (*She gasps for air*)
Marie-Therese Why not?
Bernadette The spring is not for me. (*She pauses to regain her breath*)
Alexandre Now tell them what the lady required of you. (*Prompting*) Your penance, Bernadette. Your penance!
Bernadette The lady asked for penance, mortification and prayers for sinners.

Marie-Therese What penance did you submit?
Bernadette My illness, Mother.
Josephine Now ask your questions, Sisters.
Emilienne I believe she asked for a church to be built?
Bernadette The lady said I was to tell the priests to build a chapel at the grotto, and that people were to come there in procession.
Alexandre Her wish was granted when the crypt was consecrated.
Paschal The lady?
Bernard Dalias You have mentioned very little about her.

Bernadette smiles, conserving her breath

Vincent Garros Was she beautiful?

Bernadette nods her head

Emilienne How beautiful was she?
Bernadette So beautiful that when you have seen her once you would be happy to die to see her again.
Paschal Do you remember what she looked like?
Bernadette (*touching her forehead*) She is still here.
Vincent Garros And her voice?

Bernadette appears to retreat into her memory, hearing an inner voice

Her voice, what was it like?
Bernadette I heard her voice in my heart, rather than in my ear.
Marie-Therese I believe you were given a personal message?
Bernadette Yes, Mother.
Marie-Therese What was it?
Bernadette (*slowly*) She said, "I cannot make you happy in this world, but I promise to do so in the next."

There is a small ripple of comment among the nuns

Marie-Therese Yes, but wasn't there something else? It is rumoured that you were entrusted with three secrets?
Bernadette (*softly*) Yes, Mother.
Marie-Therese And you have never revealed them?
Bernadette They wouldn't be secret if I had.
Marie-Therese But they are said to concern the whole of mankind!
Bernadette I have never said that.
Marie-Therese Others have.
Bernadette Others didn't hear them. The secrets were only for me.
Marie-Therese Then they can't have had much importance.
Bernadette They were of great importance to me, Mother.

There is a pause

Josephine Is it true that you were faced by many doubters?
Bernadette Yes, Reverend Mother. People demanded proof. Our parish priest even requested that the lady should make a wild rose bush flower.
Marie-Therese And did it?

Act I, Scene 2

Bernadette (*smiling*) No, Mother. It hadn't bloomed for years. I don't think it ever will.
Marie-Therese A pity.
Alexandre She revealed the miraculous spring instead.
Josephine Which portrays a practical nature.
Vincent Garros Is it true that they have honoured her by placing a statue in the exact place where she appeared?
Alexandre White carrera marble. So beautiful!
Bernadette (*doubtfully*) It is beautiful—(*after a pause; defensively*)—but quite unlike her.
Vincent Garros It is said to be in the pose she assumed when she revealed her name to you.

Bernadette nods

Bernard Dalias Would you show us how she stood?

Bernadette slowly folds her hands in prayer, and raises her eyes. A radiance seems to surround her

And what did she say?

There is a long pause

Bernadette I am the Immaculate Conception.

There is a silent pause, then the Angelus rings softly in the distance. Reverend Mother Josephine mounts the lectern

Josephine The angel of the Lord declared unto Mary and she conceived of the Holy Ghost.
Nuns Hail Mary, full of grace, the Lord is with thee. Blessed art thou among women, and blessed is the fruit of thy womb, Jesus. Holy Mary, Mother of God, pray for us sinners now and at the hour of our death. Amen.
Josephine Behold the handmaid of the Lord; may it be done unto me according to thy word.

The nuns repeat the Hail Mary

And the word was made flesh——

All kneel

—and dwelt among us.

The nuns repeat the Hail Mary

Pour forth, we beseech thee, O Lord, thy grace into our hearts, that we, to whom the incarnation of Christ thy son was made known by the message of an angel, may by his passion and cross, be brought to the glory of his resurrection; through the same Christ our Lord. Amen.

The prayer completed, all rise except Bernadette, who crosses herself very slowly as the others watch her

That will be all, Sisters.

The postulants file out silently

Bernadette starts to join them, but Mother Marie-Therese restrains her

Marie-Therese Now you must take leave of Mother Alexandre, my child.
Alexandre Having accomplished my duty of installing you in the Mother House, I shall return to Lourdes this evening.
Bernadette I shall miss you, Mother.
Alexandre Be happy in your vocation, my child.

Bernadette gives a small asthmatic gasp

Marie-Therese Weep if it will relieve your emotion. Trying to withhold tears only restricts the throat.
Bernadette I am not weeping, Mother.
Josephine What is it, then?
Alexandre Her exhaustion has aggravated the asthma.
Josephine I had feared that.
Bernadette It is nothing, Reverend Mother.
Josephine If it is nothing, you must control it. A house of religion is run to a precise pattern. Any indisposition can flaw its efficiency.

Bernadette straightens herself and tries to control her breathing, which only intensifies the asthma

Bernadette Yes, Reverend Mother.
Alexandre Good-bye, my child. It will please your family to know that you have settled down so well.

Bernadette and Mother Alexandre embrace

Mother Josephine and Mother Alexandre leave

Bernadette gazes after them wistfully

Marie-Therese I have listened to your story with interest.
Bernadette Thank you, Mother.
Marie-Therese I have always had a special devotion to the Blessed Virgin. All my life I have had a premonition—more than premonition—a definite knowledge that she would grace me with a particular mission. I have waited long, my daughter. You have been more fortunate.
Bernadette I did nothing to deserve so great a privilege.
Marie-Therese However, there are several points in your story which I find disturbing, as others have, I believe?

Bernadette nods gravely

You have a way of drawing a veil over certain aspects which might suspend belief.

Act I, Scene 2

Bernadette I can only tell what happened, Mother. The choice of believing or disbelieving depends on the listener.
Marie-Therese Don't misunderstand me. I do not criticize your story, but rather your way of telling it.
Bernadette As I have been forbidden to talk about it again, there will be no further chance of displeasing you, Mother.
Marie-Therese You understand that as Mistress of Novices, I am your immediate superior?
Bernadette Yes, Mother.
Marie-Therese I want to give you all the help in my power. I want you to find great happiness.
Bernadette I have found that already.
Marie-Therese Then I shall help you to increase it, if you let me.
Bernadette Thank you, Mother. I am grateful to you.
Marie-Therese From today you must forget your life in the world, all the ties you had there, and the people who were close to you. You will miss them at first. We all do.
Bernadette I shall miss my family, I know.
Marie-Therese We are now your family, and we rejoice to have a new sister—a sister we shall love and care for, and share our lives with. But you must co-operate with us, my child.
Bernadette Most willingly, Mother.
Marie-Therese Then you will understand that only with your complete confidence can I guide your vocation. Never be afraid to come to me with any doubts you may have—we all have doubts at times, but so often they are due to false pride, believing that we know better than our superiors. Do you understand, my child?

Bernadette nods

And when I summon you for an interview, you will tell me all I ask you. Any questions that I put to you, you must answer.

Bernadette gasps for air

You will trust me as your own mother, to whom I believe you were very close . . .
Bernadette (*gasping*) Mother . . .
Marie-Therese You will tell me if ever you are unhappy, what your feelings are toward your fellow postulants, whether there are any amongst them toward whom you feel particularly drawn. Be entirely open. No secrets. No private desires. Nothing.

Bernadette claws at the top of her dress in order to breathe more freely

Your asthma, my child. I believe this is an affliction which is aggravated by nervousness. You have no reason to feel uneasy in my presence, have you?

Bernadette breathlessly shakes her head

Too much can be made of illness. It is a form of self-indulgence and must not be encouraged.

Bernadette attempts to control her breathing, she appears to have a momentary calm

There, that is better already.

Bernadette nods agreement

(*Beginning to leave*) And so—God bless you. Think over what I have told you, my child, for that is the only way to find joy and fulfilment in the new life you have chosen. Do you understand?

Bernadette nods her head in agreement, and has a fit of coughing, as the Lights cross-fade on to the two Readers

During the reading the Nuns set the office scene

LINKING SCENE

First Reader Community Journal. July nineteenth, eighteen hundred and sixty-six. Word has leaked out that Bernadette Soubirous has joined the community. Each day pilgrims arrive in great crowds to ask for her. Reverend Mother Josephine firmly rejects all proposals to see or interview her.

Second Reader July twenty-ninth. The Feast of St Martha, patroness of the congregation. Together with the other postulants, Bernadette Soubirous has today completed the ceremony of clothing. After an address by Bishop Forcade, the postulants were given their novices veils and their names in religion. Mother Marie-Therese has chosen for Bernadette the name of Marie-Bernard. Mother Marie-Therese thought it appropriate that she should have the name of the Blessed Virgin plus that of her patron, St Bernard.

First Reader October twenty-fifth. In the last three months Sister Marie-Bernard's health has deteriorated, considerably. She is now seriously ill.

Second Reader October twenty-sixth, eighteen hundred and sixty-six. Sister Marie-Bernard's condition is now a matter for grave concern. She has been administered the Sacrament of Extreme Unction.

The Lights cross-fade on to the office set

SCENE 3

Mother Josephine's study

Mother Josephine sits at her desk. Mother Marie-Therese enters in agitation

Marie-Therese What can be detaining his Lordship?
Josephine Patience, Mother. Try to keep calm.

Act I, Scene 3

Marie-Therese The novices are maintaining a continuous vigil. I have insisted on that.
Josephine I cannot think your insistence was necessary. Sister Marie-Bernard's life is surely the loving concern of us all.

There is a tap at the door

Come in.

Sister Emilienne enters. She is upset and close to tears

Emilienne Mother . . .
Josephine What is it, Sister? Why have you left her bedside?
Emilienne Forgive me, Reverend Mother. I was looking for Mother Marie-Therese.
Marie-Therese What is it, Sister?
Emilienne She is in such agony. Can nothing be done?
Josephine The doctor is with her. Sister Marie-Bernard is in good hands.
Emilienne (*with a trace of hysteria*) Couldn't we summon another doctor?
Josephine (*rising*) Sister Emilienne! Doctor St Cyr will do all he is able. We do not question his authority at any time.
Emilienne But her haemorrhage—you haven't seen her, Reverend Mother! She cannot breathe!
Josephine (*interrupting*) That is enough! Control yourself, Sister!
Marie-Therese (*to Josephine*) Please, Reverend Mother . . . (*She takes Emilienne's arm and leads her across the room. Firmly but gently*) Sister, are you so weak that you falter at the first ordeal? Are you going to make a poor nurse as well as a poor nun? Is that all my teaching has done for you?
Emilienne But, we are so powerless . . .
Marie-Therese Never, Sister. Never. We have the greatest power of all at our command. The power of prayer.
Emilienne Yes—but it is so difficult . . .
Marie-Therese Would you deny her that power at this moment when she needs it most? Did the Holy Women of Calvary turn their backs on Our Lord's agony?
Emilienne (*after a pause*) Forgive me, Mother.
Marie-Therese Now, go back and offer your rosary with the other Sisters. Commend Sister Marie-Bernard's suffering into the hands of Christ and Our Blessed Lady. Offer your weakness as a penance and gain strength from it.
Emilienne (*going toward the door*) Thank you, Mother Marie-Therese. (*To Josephine*) Forgive my intrusion, Reverend Mother.

Emilienne exits

Marie-Therese I apologize for usurping your authority in your own office, Reverend Mother.
Josephine (*smiling*) This time you were justified. You were admirable.

Mother Marie-Therese moves up stage

Marie-Therese (*agitatedly*) The Last Rites were administered over an hour ago. If he doesn't arrive soon he will be too late.
Josephine This nervousness is so unlike you. The doctor will advise us when the end is imminent.
Marie-Therese Forgive me, Reverend Mother.
Josephine Is your own health satisfactory?
Marie-Therese There is nothing to complain of.
Josephine Since the girl's arrival I have noticed a distinct change in you.
Marie-Therese I am unaware of it.
Josephine An obsessive preoccupation with her.
Marie-Therese I am not aware that it has ever been obsessive.
Josephine Possessive, perhaps?
Marie-Therese We have been entrusted with the care of a special soul. To refine it has been my responsibility.
Josephine The responsibility of us all, I think.
Marie-Therese I cannot help but feel personally answerable, Reverend Mother—as I do for all my novices. Should she die now, my task will be incomplete.
Josephine No-one can ever question your diligence. That you may be unable to fulfil your mission could be God's will.
Marie-Therese There is still so much to be done—so much! (*She moves away, tautly*)
Josephine (*after a slight pause*) Her progress has satisfied you?
Marie-Therese (*evasively*) She followed the Rule punctiliously.
Josephine (*insistently*) Did her progress satisfy you?
Marie-Therese She was unassuming, pious, devoted, orderly.
Josephine Yet you seem disappointed?
Marie-Therese Reverend Mother, in all my experience of spiritual guidance I have never come across a case like this.
Josephine But you reported her behaviour as being exemplary.
Marie-Therese Despite her virtues there has been a stubbornness and touchiness which has been insurmountable.
Josephine (*with a gesture of dismissal*) Merely traits of the natural character.
Marie-Therese But she clings to them.
Josephine In a postulant less supernaturally endowed, would you expect the natural character to have been eradicated so quickly?
Marie-Therese No, Reverend Mother.
Josephine Then there seems little cause for your concern.
Marie-Therese But there is! There is much to concern me. When I interview her, and invite her to disclose her spiritual doubts, she merely smiles at me.
Josephine I have noticed that smile.
Marie-Therese There is something mysterious about it, secret. One would almost call it sly if one didn't know her. But it doesn't make my task of solving her doubts any easier.

Act I, Scene 3

Josephine Mother Marie-Therese, she is unlikely to have any doubts at this stage of her vocation.
Marie-Therese But I cannot reach her. I try most earnestly but there is a complete and utter lack of contact between us.
Josephine Perhaps you try too hard.
Marie-Therese To guide her I have to know her intimately.
Josephine There might not be any more to know.
Marie-Therese There must be. I have to know.
Josephine (*casually, after a pause*) Mother, is there any doubt in your mind?
Marie-Therese Doubt?
Josephine Of her true vocation.
Marie-Therese As a novice she is an example to us all. But as a confidante of the Blessed Virgin she leaves much to be desired.
Josephine I hope you are not presuming to dictate to whom Our Lady should appear, and to whom she should not appear!
Marie-Therese That was not my intention, Reverend Mother. I was merely speculating that there are others who appear to be more worthy.
Josephine Your speculation lacks charity. Why not accept what is offered you?
Marie-Therese I shall continue to pray for enlightenment. I shall mortify my body until I know the truth. I have to penetrate that soul.

There is a knock at the door

Josephine Death may have succeeded where we have failed, Reverend Mother. Come in.

Father Douce, the chaplain to the Mother House, enters

Douce Is there no sign of his Lordship?
Josephine No, Father. How is she?
Douce She is sinking fast.

Marie-Therese moves towards the door

Wait, Mother—she has asked to be granted the privilege of taking her final vows.
Marie-Therese To grant such a request is unprecedented! She has been in the novitiate for only three months!
Josephine (*after a moment's consideration*) Father Douce, as the end is near I consider it right to grant her request.
Marie-Therese Reverend Mother.
Josephine Will you preside at the ceremony at once, Father.
Douce His Lordship desires that privilege for himself.
Josephine If his Lordship is not here she may die unprofessed.
Marie-Therese The girl is not ready! I cannot agree!
Josephine In the name of humanity we are granting a dying wish. Father, I shall take full responsibility for your presiding in his Lordship's absence.

There is another knock at the door and Sister Emilienne enters

Emilienne Mother Josephine.
Josephine Is it over?
Emilienne No, Reverend Mother. But the doctor has summoned you urgently.

The Bishop of Nevers appears in the doorway

Bishop I came as soon as I received your message, Reverend Mother. Am I too late?
Josephine Thank God you have arrived in time, your Lordship. Please follow me.

Mother Josephine exits, followed by the others

The Lights fade to semi Black-Out. The murmured Litany of Our Lady is heard coming from the chapel

The Nuns file on and change the furniture from the office to the infirmary

The Lights fade up when the change is complete

Scene 4

The Infirmary. There is a fireplace with a statue of the Virgin Mary on the mantelpiece

Bernadette is propped up in bed, gasping for breath. Two novices, Sister Bernard Dalias and Sister Paschal kneel in prayer beside the bed. Sister Vincent Garros stands holding a folded veil, a crucifix, a rosary, manual and rule book. The Doctor is in attendance

Mother Josephine, Mother Marie-Therese, the Bishop and Father Douce enter

Bishop Can you hear me, my child?

Bernadette barely inclines her head

I believe you wish to profess your vows?

Bernadette makes an effort to raise herself but sinks back on the pillows

I am here to receive your profession, Sister.
Bernadette (*in a whisper*) No—strength . . .
Bishop I shall pronounce the formula. It will be sufficient for you to answer Amen. Can you hear me?

Act I, Scene 4

Bernadette gives a small nod of affirmation

> I, Sister Marie-Bernard, wishing to consecrate myself in the service of God, vow poverty, chastity and obedience in the Rules of the Congregation, approved by the Sovereign Pontiff. I beg our Lord Jesus Christ, by the intercession of the Most Blessed Virgin, to grant me the grace to fulfil these promises.

Bernadette Amen.

Mother Josephine spreads the veil over the girl's head. Mother Marie-Therese slips the crucifix between her fingers and arranges the rosary and rule book on her bed. Bernadette appears to fall into a coma

Bishop (*making the sign of the cross*) Benedicat vos omnipotens deus, Pater et filius et spiritus sanctus. Amen. Pray for me, Sister Marie-Bernard.

Mother Josephine kisses Bernadette's forehead then leads the Bishop out

Father Douce and the Nuns repeat the Hail Mary

Marie-Therese Doctor?
Doctor There can be no change now.
Marie-Therese Is she in pain?
Doctor I cannot understand how she has withstood it for so long.
Marie-Therese Her entire life has been a battle against poverty and disease.
Doctor Then defeat will be welcome.

Mother Marie-Therese sits at the bedside

> You are tired, Mother.

Marie-Therese My eyelids feel heavy and inflamed.
Doctor I advise you to rest. I shall stay till the end.
Marie-Therese You have worked long and hard, Doctor. If you are convinced that no more can be done, then I offer you the same advice. I shall keep vigil all night if needs be.
Bernadette (*softly, without strain*) That will not be necessary, Mother.

The Doctor and Marie-Therese move towards her in astonishment. The Novices cease praying and slowly look up

> I shall not die tonight.

The Doctor sounds her chest with a stethoscope

Marie-Therese Doctor, what has happened?
Bernadette I reached there, Mother. But they weren't ready for me.
Doctor The congestion appears to have dispersed.
Bernadette I am better, Doctor.
Marie-Therese Sister Emilienne! Summon the Mother-General immediately.

Emilienne exits

Doctor Her pulse is normal.
Marie-Therese (*accusing*) You had us believe the child was dying!
Doctor She was, Mother.
Marie-Therese Could you have diagnosed wrongly?
Doctor A trained eye is not necessary to diagnose imminent death.
Marie-Therese (*crossing herself*) Then it is a miracle!
Doctor It is not given to my calling to confirm so extravagant a diagnosis.
Marie-Therese Nor is it within your province to deny it!
Doctor This patient has a history of sudden recovery, but I did not believe her records until now.
Marie-Therese Then a series of miracles have been perpetrated upon her!

Mother Josephine hurries in, followed by Sister Emilienne

Josephine What has happened?
Marie-Therese A miracle, Reverend Mother!
Josephine The facts, Doctor.
Doctor The patient appears to have recovered.
Josephine But is this possible?
Doctor Her pulse is normal. Her respiratory tubes are clear.
Josephine Doctor, ten minutes ago . . .
Doctor She was dying, Reverend Mother. I have no doubt of it.
Josephine This incredible change . . .
Doctor It has happened before. You know her medical history.

Josephine feels Bernadette's forehead

Josephine Her brow is cool.
Doctor Believe me, there is no longer any immediate danger.

Mother Josephine's relief expresses itself in anger

Josephine (*to Bernadette*) Did you allow us to summon his Lordship at this unearthly hour of the night for nothing?
Bernadette I thought I was dying, Reverend Mother.
Josephine You allowed yourself to become the centre of attention!
Bernadette I wished to die professed.
Josephine And so you took your vows under false pretences!
Bernadette Oh, no, Reverend Mother.
Josephine Vows taken *in articulo mortis* are due for renewal a year after the patient's recovery. (*As though scolding a naughty child*) If you aren't dead by the morning, I'll take your veil away and return you to the novitiate!
Bernadette (*sincerely*) I'll do my best, Reverend Mother.

Mother Josephine angrily leaves the room followed by the Novices

Doctor You must rest, Sister.

Act I, Scene 4

Bernadette strokes her veil with awe. She offers her crucifix to Mother Marie-Therese

Bernadette See how beautiful my crucifix is, Mother. Sister Vincent, look at my rule book.

Vincent Garros (*gently*) Oh, what a little thief you are.

Bernadette Thief?

Vincent Garros Getting it under false pretences.

Bernadette Thief, perhaps. But they're mine and nobody can take them away from me. I belong to the Community now. I belong to the Community, and they'll never be able to dismiss me. Not as long as I live.

Mother Marie-Therese freezes and stares at her

Marie-Therese (*after a pause*) The time has come for you and I to become better acquainted, Sister Marie-Bernard.

Doctor The patient must rest now.

Marie-Therese Now that you are one of us we'll have to hammer that soul into shape.

Bernadette Strike the hammer gently, Mother.

Bernadette sinks back on to her pillow. The Lights cross-fade on to the Readers

During the cross-fade the Doctor and Nuns remove the Infirmary furniture and set the Bishop's chair

Linking Scene

First Reader Community Journal. October thirteenth, eighteen hundred and sixty-seven. Today the Novices take their final vows—accompanied by Sister Marie-Bernard, who will renew the vows previously taken by her *in articulo mortis.*

During the above, two Nuns enter carrying bunches of white flowers. Mother Josephine enters from another part and goes to the Bishop's chair. Mother Alexandre enters with Sister Marthe Fores. A Nun (Louise Cartier) enters: she is acting as a stand-in for Bernadette (who is completing her quick change) She goes to the front of the Bishop's chair. Mother Josephine puts a black nun's veil on her head, then the Nun backs away two steps and prostrates herself on the floor.

Second Reader Owing to her unique history, it has been decided to retain Sister Marie-Bernard at Nevers, but due to the danger of her pride becoming inflated, the reason for her retention will be withheld from her.

The Lights cross-fade on to the main set. Mother Josephine moves away from the chair

Scene 5

The Great Hall of the Novitiate

Mother Marie-Therese enters from one side, Father Douce and the Bishop from the other, the Bishop preceding. He sits in his chair. The Postulants process in a line across the front of the stage and bow to the Bishop, then form a row. The order of procession is: Sister Bernard Dalias, Bernadette, Sister Paschal, Sister Emilienne, Sister Vincent Garros

Josephine My daughters, this morning you have become professed. As you are now full members of the community your days of preparation must be utilized in practice. In the usual custom of this house, his Lordship will present you with your letters of appointment. We hope you will fulfil the trust we have in you. (*With a nod to Mother Marie-Therese*) Please proceed, Mother.

Marie-Therese calls out the names of the nuns: Vincent Garros, Emilienne Duboe, Stanislas Paschal, Bernard Dalias. They each go to the Bishop, who hands them their letters of appointment. Each kneels before him, kisses the letter, then goes to Josephine, who hands them their rule books. They then make a line up and down the stage. Finally only Bernadette is the only nun left in her original position. She looks at the Bishop with expectation

Bishop We appear to be one letter short, Reverend Mother.
Josephine That is all, your Lordship. Will you come to the refectory now?
Bishop But what duty has been allotted to Sister Marie-Bernard?

Bernadette looks eagerly from the Bishop to Mother Josephine

Marie-Therese Sister Marie-Bernard has no assignment, your Lordship.
Bishop Isn't that a little irregular?
Marie-Therese Irregular perhaps, your Lordship. But Sister Marie-Bernard is good for nothing.

Bernadette remains frozen and unresponsive. There is a small shocked ripple among the Nuns

Bishop But what do you intend to do with her?
Josephine We were awaiting your suggestion, your Lordship.
Marie-Therese She'd be a burden to any house we sent her to.
Bishop (*beckoning her over*) My daughter.

Bernadette goes towards the Bishop

So you are of no use to the community, Sister?
Bernadette No, your Lordship.
Bishop And how do you know that?
Bernadette Mother Marie-Therese says so.
Bishop And do you believe her?
Bernadette I have no reason to disbelieve her.

Act I, Scene 5

Bishop But if you are so useless, what was the point of your entering the community?
Bernadette My Lord, do you remember the day you first approached me in Lourdes regarding the possibility of my entering the religious life?
Bishop Yes.
Bernadette Well, do you remember what you said when I told you that apart from domestic work I was a complete dunce?
Bishop No, my child.
Bernadette You said it did not matter.
Bishop (*taken aback*) Did I? Well—er—neither it does. No doubt you could fetch and carry in the kitchens. And there is much unskilled work in the infirmary. You could do that, couldn't you?
Bernadette I could try, your Lordship.
Bishop (*turning to Mother Josephine*) I suppose we could keep her here for a while, Mother Josephine?
Josephine (*moving toward the door*) We have no alternative, your Lordship.
Bishop (*to Bernadette*) As soon as you prove yourself capable of doing something useful, we'll give you a more responsible appointment.
Marie-Therese I can see we are to have the pleasure of Sister Marie-Bernard's company for a good many years to come.
Bishop Not necessarily, Mother.
Marie-Therese We could never impose her on anyone else.
Bishop (*thoughtfully looking at Bernadette*) Sister Marie-Bernard, I assign to you the post of praying.
Bernadette Praying, your Lordship?
Bishop Yes, praying.
Bernadette But that isn't an assignment, your Lordship. I always pray.
Bishop Then intensify your prayers.

Bernadette kisses the Bishop's ring, nods, and wanders disappointedly to join the other Nuns

Josephine Your Lordship, will you take your refreshment now?
Bishop Thank you, Mother Josephine.

Mother Josephine and the Bishop leave, followed by Mother Marie-Therese

The newly professed Nuns form a group. Bernadette stands dejectedly apart from them

Emilienne What is your appointment, Sister?
Vincent Garros I am to remain in the Mother House until I have completed my training as a nurse.
Emilienne And I, too.
Bernard Dalias (*teasing*) Oh, I am glad to be leaving, Sister. If I were ill, you are the last person I should like to have nursing me.
Emilienne What do you mean?

Bernard Dalias You are so sensitive I'd probably end up by nursing you!
Vincent Garros Don't be such a tease, Sister. Sister Emilienne will be very efficient. (*Turning to Paschal*) Where are you going, Sister?
Paschal Far away from Mother Marie-Therese, thank goodness. Think of me when next you're given a penance, Sister Vincent.
Vincent Garros I'm no longer her novice. Thank goodness.
Emilienne Oh, you're all too harsh on Mother Marie-Therese!
Paschal Not nearly as harsh as she's been to us. Since my inception I've kissed the floor so many times, I know it as well as the palm of my hand!
Emilienne I'd hardly call them unwarranted penances, Sister.
Bernard Dalias I've always found her so patient and wise.
Vincent Garros Then you are an exception, Sister.
Emilienne Oh, nonsense, Sister Vincent. She has been a great help to me in my vocation.
Vincent Garros Then I must be the exception.
Bernard Dalias Even Sister Anastasie says that without Mother Marie-Therese's patience, she would have renounced her vocation long ago.
Paschal Whatever happened to Sister Anastasie?
Bernard Dalias She has already left for the House of Nervous Disorders in Tarbes.
Vincent Garros So much for Mother Marie-Therese's patience.
Paschal She always seemed so composed.
Bernard Dalias Not as an inmate, Sister! She is to be Assistant Infirmarian.
Paschal Oh, how I envy her! I have always had an affinity for the sick, but Mother Marie-Therese thought I was better suited to teaching.
Bernard Dalias I envy the children you teach, Sister.
Paschal They may not learn much, but at least they won't have penances imposed on them. Imagine, I shall be with them tomorrow morning!
Vincent Garros Where have you been assigned, Sister?
Paschal Lourdes.

There is a pause, as, suddenly remembering, they turn towards Bernadette

Bernadette You are most fortunate, Sister.
Paschal Were it in my power I would willingly change assignments with you.
Bernadette I shall never return there.
Vincent Garros We are sorry for the humiliation you have endured today, Sister.
Bernadette Public humiliation helps suppress the natural side of one's character.
Vincent Garros But it was so unjust!
Bernard Dalias They called you good for nothing.
Paschal You are more practical than any of us.
Emilienne Your needlework is exquisite!
Bernadette Sisters, we are trained to do good works. To teach and nurse. I am no good at any of these.

Act I, Scene 5

Paschal In your place today, I would have been unable to suppress my feelings towards Mother Marie-Therese.
Bernard Dalias (*reprimanding*) Sister!
Vincent Garros I would have screamed at her!
Bernard Dalias Sister Vincent Garros, your sentiments are unworthy of your vocation.
Bernadette Sisters, we must try and see God in our superiors at all times.

Mother Marie-Therese enters and listens to the Nuns

But I'll tell you a secret. Sometimes I boil inside.

The Nuns laughingly protest

But only inside, I try not to let it show. I always submit, come what may.
Bernard Dalias Your conquest of the natural character is an example to us all.
Bernadette (*laughing*) If that is true, which I doubt, then perhaps I was given the grace of greater effort because I had more to overcome.
Marie-Therese Sister Marie-Bernard! Kiss the floor!

Bernadette immediately kneels and kisses the floor. The appalled Nuns disperse

Sisters, make haste! Some of you have trains to catch. Those remaining have the celebratory meal to attend. Sister Marie Vincent has baked a cake specially for the occasion! Please hurry!

The Nuns leave

Bernadette starts to follow them

Not you, Sister Marie-Bernard!
Bernadette You wish to see me, Mother?
Marie-Therese Why did you accept my penance so readily?
Bernadette Because it was for the good of my soul.
Marie-Therese And why were you given the penance in the first place?
Bernadette (*bewildered*) I don't know . . .
Marie-Therese Then how do you know it was for the good of your soul?
Bernadette Because you wouldn't have given it to me otherwise, Mother.
Marie-Therese I gave it to you because you always try to be the centre of attention.
Bernadette Oh, no . . .
Marie-Therese Always trying to impose yourself on the other Sisters. What were you talking about?
Bernadette They were discussing their appointments.
Marie-Therese I didn't ask what they were discussing. What were you telling them?
Bernadette Nothing, Mother.
Marie-Therese Evasiveness will be your downfall.

Bernadette (*irritated*) Oh, Mother Marie-Therese.
Marie-Therese Do another penance!
Bernadette (*astonished*) What for?
Marie-Therese Do you question my authority?

Bernadette kisses the floor

Bernadette It would be beneficial if I knew why I was doing a penance.
Marie-Therese That was for touchiness. The first was for self-love.
Bernadette I am guilty of touchiness, Mother. I try to overcome it.
Marie-Therese Was that an implication that you are free of self-love?
Bernadette My life is a constant battle against it.
Marie-Therese (*softening*) That is as it should be, my child.
Bernadette We are all guilty of self-love, Mother. But I try to remember your teaching that it only dies with the body.
Marie-Therese (*her antagonism re-aroused*) You are always quick with the pert reply! I try to understand you, Sister, but you do nothing to simplify my task.
Bernadette There is nothing to understand, but what you see before you.
Marie-Therese What I see before me is someone piously evasive. Your trouble is that you always have too much to say at the wrong time. Whenever I invite you to unburden yourself, you stand mute.
Bernadette I search my heart in the hope of finding something to discuss, Mother, because I know it will please you. But my heart is free of doubt and spiritual anxiety. There is never anything to unburden.
Marie-Therese Yet you always find enough to say to the other Sisters.
Bernadette But that is just talk.
Marie-Therese Then why not talk to me?
Bernadette I always answer your questions.
Marie-Therese That is not the same thing! You never confide in me!
Bernadette I don't understand what you would have me confide!
Marie-Therese (*after a pause*) Do you have any personal prejudice against me?
Bernadette No.
Marie-Therese Would you perhaps have unfolded more readily to some other person?
Bernadette There is no more to unfold.
Marie-Therese I have to know!
Bernadette What is there to know?
Marie-Therese Tell me!

Mother Marie-Therese advances slowly on Bernadette

Bernadette Mother, please . . .
Marie-Therese (*cornering her*) Tell me what really happened at Lourdes!

Bernadette tries to side-step, but Mother Marie-Therese blocks her exit

If the Holy Father wanted to know, would you tell him?
Bernadette (*with a small cry of anguish*) What, Mother Marie-Therese? What would he want to know that I haven't already told you?

Act I, Scene 5

Marie-Therese The three secrets!

There is a pause

Bernadette (*solemnly, with a new strength*) No.
Marie-Therese (*shocked*) You would even deny the Holy Father?
Bernadette (*extricating herself*) The Holy Father wouldn't ask me such a question, Mother. He knows it is of no concern to him.
Marie-Therese (*advancing on her*) Isn't it?

Sister Marthe Fores and Sister Paschal enter followed by a small group of Nuns. Both Sisters wear cloaks over their habits. Sister Paschal carries a travelling bag and an umbrella

Marthe Fores Mother Marie-Therese, Sister Paschal is leaving for Lourdes.

Mother Marie-Therese crosses to Paschal and kisses her on both cheeks

Marie-Therese God bless you, Sister.
Paschal Thank you, Mother. Good-bye, Sister Marie-Bernard. I shall be able to tell your family that you are well again.
Bernadette Remember me.
Marthe Fores Come, Sister! Your train will leave you behind!
Paschal Good-bye, Sisters! God bless you all!

Bernadette turns away as if to shut out any thoughts of Lourdes

The Nuns go off, chattering among themselves

Marie-Therese Now that you are professed, you will no longer be under my personal jurisdiction—but should you ever feel the need to share your secrets—should you ever feel the weight of them too heavy on your soul—remember, I am here . . .
Bernadette I cannot reveal the secrets to any person!
Marie-Therese I shall be watching—and waiting . . .
Bernadette For what?
Marie-Therese For the moment when you will turn to me.

Mother Marie-Therese goes off swiftly

Bernadette Oh, God, help me—help me . . . !

The CURTAIN *falls slowly*

ACT II

The two Readers are at their lecterns

Second Reader The Community Journal, January first, eighteen hundred and sixty-eight. Sister Marie-Bernard has been appointed to the office of Assistant Infirmarian. But her duties are confined to the general cleanliness of the wards.
First Reader December tenth, eighteen-sixty-eight. The sad news of the death of the mother of Sister Marie-Bernard has reached us. When informed of her mother's death the good sister collapsed from the enormity of her grief. Upon revival, she continued her duties without mentioning the matter again.
Second Reader Although it was agreed that she was to have no contact with the patients, Sister Marthe Fores, the Infirmarian, states that Sister Marie-Bernard alone is capable of comforting the more serious cases.

The Lights cross-fade to the Infirmary

SCENE 1

The Infirmary

The room is lit by an overhead lamp which casts a shadowy pool of light to form the main acting area. The voices of the patients are heard off stage. From each wing we can see the end of an iron bed. A large medicine cabinet on castors stands in between the ends of the beds

First Patient (*off*) Sister Marie-Bernard!

Bernadette enters and goes to the bed of the patient who called. There is evidence of a slight limp. She carries a pail and scrubbing brush

I am frightened.

Bernadette There is nothing to fear. You are recovering.
First Patient (*off*) I nearly died.
Bernadette We all have to die some day.
First Patient (*off*) Don't you fear death?
Bernadette No.
Second Patient (*off*) Sister Marie-Bernard, I am in pain.

Bernadette crosses to the other side

Bernadette We must suffer a little for God, Sister. He suffered so much for us.

Act II, Scene 1

First Patient (*off*) Sister, please straighten my pillow.
Bernadette I'm coming. (*She starts to move back towards the First Patient*)
Third Patient (*off*) Sister, Marie-Bernard.
Bernadette One moment. I only have two hands.
Third Patient (*off*) Sister, I am thirsty.
Bernadette There's fresh water by your bed. Try to sleep. (*She watches the patient for a moment, then, as she starts to clean the floor, begins very softly to sing, to the tune of "Frère Jacques"*)

> Sister Paula, Sister Paula,
> Go to sleep, go to sleep.
> Sleep until the bells ring,
> Sleep until the bells ring,
> Ding, dang, dong.

A Patient (*very softly*) Ding, dang, dong.
Bernadette (*moving towards the other bed*)

> Little Sisters, little Sisters,
> Angels keep, angels keep.
> Sleep until the bells ring.
> Sleep until the bells ring,
> Ding dang dong.

Sister Marthe Fores enters. She is fluttery and over-excited

Marthe Fores Sister Marie-Bernard! You haven't finished the floor yet! Hurry up, we haven't all day. Mother-General will be making her rounds soon!

A bell rings. Bernadette starts to answer it

Is that Sister Lescure ringing? Have you changed her dressings?
Bernadette Not yet, Sister.
Marthe Fores What have you been doing?
First Patient (*off*) Water!
Bernadette One moment, I'm coming.
Marthe Fores Mother-General on her way, and you wasting time talking to the patients! (*Calling*) Sister Vincent Garros! (*Moving back to Bernadette*) Because of your sloth another sister will have to perform your duties.

Sister Vincent Garros enters

Sister Vincent, *you'll* have to change Sister Lescure's dressings.
Vincent Garros (*distastefully*) Oh—please . . .
Marthe Fores Hurry up! We are behind times!
Vincent Garros Her wound is so repulsive.
Marthe Fores Then be grateful you aren't afflicted with it.

Vincent Garros She is even surrounded by screens so that no-one may see her.
Bernadette Sister Vincent, if you comfort Sister Lescure I will attend to her dressing as soon as I have finished the floor.
Marthe Fores She doesn't need comforting. She needs her bed changed!
Bernadette But until it is, she will be content to know that she isn't being neglected.

Sister Vincent Garros goes off towards Sister Lescure's bed.
Sister Emilienne enters

Emilienne Sister Marthe, the Mother-General has summoned you.
Marthe Fores We'll all be reprimanded! She's heard of the disorder and it will be penances all round!
Bernadette (*soothingly*) Take a deep breath to compose yourself, Sister. Everything will be in order by the time of the inspection.
Marthe Fores (*going*) Sister Emilienne, the kettles need filling and the breakfast trays are *not* as Reverend Mother likes them to be—and where are Sister Lescure's special bandages . . . ?

Sister Marthe Fores and Sister Emilienne go off

Bernadette resumes her cleaning
Sister Vincent returns from Sister Lescure's bed.

Mother Josephine enters, aided by a stick, unseen by the others

Vincent Garros Sister Lescure is sleeping.
Bernadette It is better that she rests. I'll change her dressings when she wakes.
Vincent Garros Thank you, Sister.

Sister Vincent-Garros goes off

Josephine Since when was changing Sister Lescure's dressing your duty, Sister?
Bernadette Mother . . . (*She rises, startled*)
Josephine Where is Sister Marthe Fores?
Bernadette You summoned her, Reverend Mother.
Josephine I?
Bernadette So I understood. Some while ago.
Josephine And you have elected to deputize for her?
Bernadette I thought . . .
Josephine The Rule does not require an Assistant Infirmarian to think.
Bernadette No, Reverend Mother. Will you begin your tour of inspection now?
Josephine That will not be my duty tonight. The doctor has forced me to rest for a while. I came to wish my fellow patients a good night before I retired.

Act II, Scene 1

Bernadette (*moving towards Sister Lescure's cubicle*) Sister Lescure . . .

Bernadette signs to Josephine that the patient is sleeping and the Reverend Mother makes the sign of the cross over the bed

(*Indicating another cubicle*) Sister François . . .
Josephine God bless you, Sister.
Second Patient (*off*) God bless you, Reverend Mother.
Bernadette (*moving towards another cubicle*) Sister Paula . . .
Josephine Sister, why are you limping?
Bernadette It is nothing, Reverend Mother.
Josephine One does not limp for nothing, Sister.
Bernadette It's only my knee, Reverend Mother.
Josephine Show me.

Bernadette returns and lifts her skirt. The knee is shielded from our view. Mother Josephine looks at the knee, then stares hard at Bernadette

Has the Doctor inspected this?
Bernadette It is of no consequence.
Josephine But has nobody else noticed your limp?
Bernadette Mother Marie-Therese was kind enough to remark on it.
Josephine What did she say?
Bernadette She told me to walk properly. She said one only limped to attract attention to one's self. (*She picks up the pail*)
Josephine (*controlling her shock*) Your heavy duties must be curtailed.
Bernadette But the floors, Reverend Mother.
Josephine There are other capable sisters.

Mother Josephine goes off slowly

Bernadette limps painfully up stage and stares off, as if through a window, breathing deeply

Sister Vincent Garros enters

Vincent Garros Mother Josephine has asked me to relieve you, Sister.

Bernadette fails to respond, but continues to stare out of the window

Are you tired, Sister?
Bernadette (*leaving the "window"*) No.
Vincent Garros Then are you unwell?
Bernadette I was looking at the poplars out there. They remind me so much of Lourdes.
Vincent Garros You miss it very much?
Bernadette It was like heaven on earth to me. (*She coughs*) What else do we have to do?
Vincent Garros Nothing.
Bernadette Then I must find something.
Vincent Garros You overwork yourself.

Bernadette I must not be idle, Sister. (*She coughs again*)
Vincent Garros That cough is getting worse.
Bernadette I have always had it.
Vincent Garros It should have been treated when you were a child.
Bernadette When I was a child there were more important matters to be considered than coughs.
Vincent Garros What is more important than one's health?
Bernadette Bread, my dear Sister Vincent. Or the lack of it. Once my little brother was caught eating the candle scrapings from the church floor. And I can assure you it wasn't because he liked the taste of candle wax.
Vincent Garros To be guaranteed happiness in the next world is what matters. Surely that is the ultimate grace.
Bernadette It is not as easy as that.
Vincent Garros What could be easier? When one's final destination is assured, what could be more pleasant than to sit back and enjoy the journey?
Bernadette One is given instructions at the start of the journey. How one conducts one's self according to these instructions is what matters. (*Moving away*) I must polish the bedposts.
Vincent Garros You have already done so.
Bernadette The water jugs have to be replenished.
Vincent Garros Why do you avoid me?
Bernadette Oh, Sister . . .
Vincent Garros You do.
Bernadette We have work to do.
Vincent Garros Do you dislike me?

Undetected by the two nuns, Mother Marie-Therese emerges from the shadows. She listens to their conversation

Bernadette We work well together, Sister Vincent.
Vincent Garros Is that all?
Bernadette (*her arm around Sister Vincent Garros's shoulder*) You are my sister in religion, but I love you as though you were my blood sister. Working with you in the infirmary has given me the greatest happiness since entering the community. There, are you satisfied?
Marie-Therese Sister Marie-Bernard!

Startled, the two Nuns spring apart

Do a penance!

Bernadette does so, kneeling

Vincent Garros Mother! You haven't the right! She is no longer a novice!
Marie-Therese Sister Vincent Garros, report to the kitchens.
Vincent Garros The kitchens?
Marie-Therese You heard what I said.
Vincent Garros Why, Mother?

Act II, Scene 1

Marie-Therese Because I told you to.
Vincent Garros No, Mother.
Marie-Therese Kiss the floor!
Vincent Garros No.
Marie-Therese I give you one more chance before I report you.
Vincent Garros Only the Mother-General has the right to reassign a professed sister, *or* to demand a penance.
Marie-Therese (*frigid with authority*) Due to the indisposition of Mother Josephine I have this day taken over the duties and position of Mother-General of the entire community.

Sister Vincent Garros performs her penance

You are hereby relieved of your duties in the infirmary. You will report to the kitchens immediately.
Vincent Garros Yes, Mother.

Sister Vincent Garros rises and exits

Marie-Therese (*gently*) Come here, my child. Did you wonder why I reassigned Sister Vincent Garros?
Bernadette It is your privilege to do so, Mother.
Marie-Therese In a community such as ours the danger of personal attachments is always strong.

Bernadette stares at her dumbly

Your vocation worries me more than others. I have to guard it jealously.
Bernadette Thank you, Mother.
Marie-Therese Your face is drawn, Sister. Are you in pain?
Bernadette Not unduly, Mother.
Marie-Therese Do you think a change of duties might be beneficial?
Bernadette Whatever you say, Mother.
Marie-Therese (*a trace of irritation*) I am trying to help you, Sister Marie-Bernard.
Bernadette Thank you, Mother. Will you make your inspection now?

Bernadette moves away. Mother Marie-Therese follows

Marie-Therese You once told me that there was a particularly close relationship between you and your mother.
Bernadette She loved all her children equally.
Marie-Therese But she devoted more attention to you?
Bernadette An asthmatic child requires particular attention, Mother.
Marie-Therese (*drawing closer*) You still suffer from asthma.
Bernadette But I am no longer a child, and my mother is dead.
Marie-Therese I was sorry to hear it, my daughter. (*She puts her arm round Bernadette's shoulder*) Perhaps you will find it easier to confide in me now—and look on *me* as your mother . . .

Bernadette withdraws from the embrace

Bernadette My mother is dead, and my childhood died with her.

A look of hurt rejection crosses Mother Marie-Therese's face

Marie-Therese (*after a pause*) You are quite right, Sister. We should not expect dispensations in the religious life. (*She turns away*) And now we each have our duties to perform.

Mother Marie-Therese goes to the First Patient's bed, Bernadette limps towards another. Still preoccupied with Bernadette, Mother Marie-Therese turns to the patient

Marie-Therese (*to the patient*) How are you this evening, Sister?
First Patient (*off*) I am in pain, Reverend Mother. If only I could be taken to the Grotto in Lourdes . . .
Marie-Therese (*frigidly*) We can take good care of you here, Sister.
First Patient (*off; persistently*) But the spring would cure me.

Voices of patients are heard overlapping and rising in crescendo

Second Patient The lame have been made to walk . . .
Third Patient The blind can see again . . .
First Patient Have pity on us, Blessed Lady of Lourdes.
Marie-Therese (*angrily turning towards Bernadette*) Sister Marie-Bernard! Who is responsible for cleaning this corridor?
Bernadette I am, Mother.
Marie-Therese (*coldly*) Then your responsibilities appear to lie very lightly on your shoulders. Do it again!

Bernadette sinks painfully to the floor

Mother Marie-Therese leaves angrily

The Lights fade. As the scene is changed the Office is heard being sung in the chapel. Down stage, Sister Marthe Fores and a Nun cross the stage carrying blankets. From the other side Sister Paschal crosses with a set of school books. A Nun enters from either side: they meet in the middle, speak for a few moments then exit. Sister Vincent Garros and Sister Emilienne cross, carrying sheets

As this activity goes on down stage, other Nuns change the set to the office scene

When ready, Josephine enters and stands by her desk reading a small missal, and the Lights come up to full

Scene 2

Mother Josephine's office

Mother Marie-Therese enters angrily to Mother Josephine, who is reading by her desk

Act II, Scene 2

Marie-Therese Mother Josephine!
Josephine It is usual to knock, Mother.
Marie-Therese Your behaviour is unpardonable.
Josephine As unpardonable as your rude invasion of my privacy?
Marie-Therese I would like to know why you have undermined my authority, by demanding that Sister Marie-Bernard be given a medical examination!
Josephine If you have eyes use them. The girl is ill.
Marie-Therese She takes pride in flaunting her perpetual ill health. In my opinion she does not need a doctor.
Josephine And in my opinion she does.
Marie-Therese Then why couldn't she beg for one the same as anyone else?
Josephine Since when has anyone had to beg for a doctor in this house?
Marie-Therese That isn't what I meant.
Josephine Unfortunately, you did mean it. Nothing would give you greater satisfaction than to see that girl beg.
Marie-Therese (*shocked*) Reverend Mother!
Josephine Oh, I may be indisposed, but I haven't missed anything. I have watched your treatment of the girl.
Marie-Therese I have only followed the course of action agreed upon at her inception.
Josephine Had I known to what lengths you were prepared to go, I would never have given my consent.
Marie-Therese My treatment of Sister Marie-Bernard has never differed from yours.
Josephine I have never been deliberately cruel.
Marie-Therese Neither have I.
Josephine You have used her ill health to debase her.
Marie-Therese Am I being accused of prejudicial behaviour?
Josephine Once you were her champion.
Marie-Therese In the beginning I was susceptible. There were rational queries, but I wanted her to convince me. I wanted to believe.
Josephine But you don't.
Marie-Therese I can no longer contain my doubt. From time immemorial young girls have imagined they have seen things.
Josephine So you conclude the girl is deluded?
Marie-Therese Yes! Hallucinated! And I challenge a cult that is founded on hallucination!
Josephine Haven't you overlooked the one factor in favour of the girl's testimony?
Marie-Therese I have overlooked nothing.
Josephine What of the spring?
Marie-Therese (*disparagingly*) You are as aware as I am that in the Pyrenees there is a spa for every known complaint.
Josephine I also know that the grotto water contains no therapeutic substances.
Marie-Therese Which only goes to prove that the cures are performed through mass hysteria.

Josephine (*moving to her desk and sitting*) I suggest you offer that explanation to the afflicted who have been made whole. But even if you should be correct, don't forget that millions have faith in the spring. And when a substantial crumb is offered to a world starved of faith, I would not question its origins.

Marie-Therese I have no argument. Only an increasing doubt that she truly saw the Blessed Mother of God.

Josephine Then I am sorry for you. But my concern is for Sister Marie-Bernard, too. And now that you are of the belief that she is not supernaturally privileged, you will not object to her being treated with more leniency in future.

Marie-Therese Now you favour her! Our Rule, Reverend Mother, demands a uniformity of treatment.

Josephine That is all I ask.

Marie-Therese Her pride has to be subjugated. Surely you understand that.

Josephine If there was ever any danger to her pride, I am of the opinion that it no longer exists. I also know that you have questioned her privately about matters which we agreed were not to be mentioned in this house again.

Marie-Therese I had to know from her own lips what really happened at Lourdes.

Josephine The happenings there do not concern her vocation as a nun. If she has been dishonest or deceitful, it is a matter between her and her confessor. It does not concern you.

Marie-Therese It concerns the foundations upon which my faith is built.

Josephine The Church does not compel you to believe.

Marie-Therese I want to believe! But why? Why should the Blessed Virgin have appeared to her?

Josephine Did you ever ask her?

Marie-Therese I did. I considered her reply to be pert. She said that if the Blessed Virgin could have found someone more lowly she'd have chosen that one instead.

Josephine A very unassuming answer.

Marie-Therese In anyone so privileged surely there should be some manifestation of the grace bestowed? The apparition is said to have asked for penance. What penance has she offered? What mortification have we ever seen that would show us proof of such a divine request? She suffers from asthma, certainly—but this is hardly the price to pay for such a privilege. I want more than that! I want proof that her agony is greater than that to which I submit my own body—for I have stretched the capacity for suffering beyond human endurance. Let her show me abnegation and suffering which *I* have not experienced! What devotion does she have to our Blessed Mother that can match mine? My whole life has been devoted to her, and her alone . . .

Josephine Nobody denies your devotion . . .

Marie-Therese Then why believe that she was chosen above me?

Act II, Scene 2   37

Josephine (*after a pause*) It is not for us to question . . .
Marie-Therese I do question. It's time *somebody* started to question the girl!
Josephine Your doubts are your own, Mother. But in future you will treat Sister Marie-Bernard like any other sister in this house. I would go so far as to say that for both your sakes, it is preferable that you see as little of her as possible.

There is a knock at the door

Come in.

The Doctor enters

Josephine rises

Doctor The examination has been completed, Reverend Mother.
Josephine And?

The Doctor looks enquiringly at Mother Marie-Therese

Josephine Please continue, Mother Marie-Therese will wish to hear. (*She sits*)
Doctor Why wasn't I informed earlier of the condition of Sister Marie-Bernard's knee?
Marie-Therese Her knee?
Doctor Hadn't you noticed her limp?
Marie-Therese Many of us suffer from rheumatic pains, Doctor. We are taught to bear suffering.
Doctor Did anyone examine her so-called rheumatic pains?
Marie-Therese If I examined all Sister Marie-Bernard's ailments, there would be little time for my own duties.
Doctor A remark hardly befitting a Sister of Charity. If you could have spared the time, you might have saved a great deal of suffering.
Marie-Therese An examination was not considered necessary.
Doctor On whose authority?
Marie-Therese Authority never came into it, Doctor. She never asked for attention.
Doctor (*after a pause*) Sister Marie-Bernard has a tumour.

Mother Marie-Therese looks hard at him

Marie-Therese But—she never complained.
Doctor A characteristic of hers which you should be accustomed to by now.
Marie-Therese It has obviously brought her little discomfort.
Doctor Mother Marie-Therese, what intensity of pain can your mind conceive?

She stares at him

   I suggest you try and imagine the most excruciating pain possible, then magnify it many times, and you may reach an approximation of her agony. An agony which you have deliberately ignored.

Mother Marie-Therese sits down heavily. Her conscience-stricken figure is rigid. Her face impassive. Only her nervously contorted fingers express her inner anguish

The infection is of a tubercular nature. The tumour on her knee is the size of my fist. She has knelt on it to scrub floors, Reverend Mother.
Josephine Can you do anything to help her?
Doctor We can but try.
Josephine Her heavy duties have been curtailed.
Doctor But while she is able it would be beneficial to keep her occupied.
Josephine There is no other office vacant.
Doctor Then one will have to be created.
Josephine She might assist the sacristan—the duties are light. Mainly the preparation of the altar.
Doctor I shall visit her daily, Reverend Mother.
Josephine Thank you, Doctor.
Doctor The gratitude is mine. In my profession one doesn't often come across a case like this. We are trained to see only the body. Familiarity with it reduces everything to that one common denominator. But with Sister Marie-Bernard one is aware of another dimension . . .
Josephine (*drily*) We call it the soul, Doctor.
Doctor Call it what you will. To witness the emanation of holiness in her suffering would convert the hardest cynics.

Expression returns to the rigid form of Mother Marie-Therese. She slowly turns to face Mother Josephine

Marie-Therese How could I have been so blind? This physical torment is *surely* the penance required of her by our Blessed Lady! All doubt must be laid to rest now.
Doctor Unfortunately not, Mother. In the medical profession her case is still dismissed as mere mumbo-jumbo. I recently received a request for information on her from the Society of Doctors of Orne. They had held a seminar on the miracles of Lourdes. Their conclusion was that the whole affair was based on the evidence of an hallucinated child.

Mother Marie-Therese looks at him sharply

They even went so far as to surmise that the girl was being held prisoner here.
Josephine Prisoner?
Doctor To prevent her speaking further, and possibly jeopardizing the rich financial interest growing up around the grotto.
Josephine We are aware of these rumours, Doctor. They also say that Lourdes was dreamed up in Rome to revive religious fervour.
Doctor We live in a world where even the inexplicable must have an answer.
Josephine (*leading the Doctor toward the door*) And when there are no

Act II, Scene 2

answers, what easier than to create them? Thank you for your kindness, Doctor.
Doctor I'd like to see the Infirmarian before I leave.
Josephine (*leading him off*) Certainly, I'll take you to him.

Josephine leaves

Marie-Therese (*urgently*) Doctor!

The Doctor turns to her

Marie-Therese What is the Society of Doctors of Orne?
Doctor Exactly what it says, Mother. A society of distinguished doctors.
Marie-Therese Do you mean their qualifications are unsurpassed in the medical profession?
Doctor (*smiling*) I would prefer to call them the Bishops of my profession.
Marie-Therese And they said she was hallucinated?
Doctor I wouldn't let it disturb you, Mother. Even Bishops are capable of being mistaken.
Marie-Therese But what did you reply—regarding her hallucinations?
Doctor I told them in no uncertain *words* that I have been privileged to work with her. And whilst she was my infirmarian, she performed her duties to my complete satisfaction.
Marie-Therese But what did you specifically say about her being hallucinated?
Doctor I confirmed that her efficient clinical detachment does not render her in the least way liable to hysteria.
Marie-Therese (*a pause*) But you yourself admitted that doctors are sometimes fallible. Doctor, do you believe her?
Doctor (*after a pause*) I have no reason for disbelief, Mother. Have you?

The Doctor goes off

The Lights cross-fade on to the two Readers, and during the following the Nuns remove the office furniture and the Chapel scene is set

Linking Scene

First Reader Community Journal. April fourteenth, eighteen hundred and seventy-eight. The mild spring weather has been kind to Sister Marie-Bernard's health. Her asthmatic attacks have been fewer, and even the pain in her knee has eased.

Bernadette, Sister Vincent Garros and Sister Emilienne enter with chairs. They sit and sew

Both physically and mentally Sister Marie-Bernard is enjoying a tranquillity she has not known for some years.

SEWING SONG (Tune: *Kola*)
Bernadette (*singing softly*)
Mary wore a crown of roses
Mary wore a gown of blue.
Mary sang a song to her baby
"Jesus, I'm sewing a bonnet for you."

"Golden lilies, snowy white daisies,
Lavender, rosemary, violets blue,
I'm sewing my love into this little bonnet,
Sewing a garden of flowers for you."

Chorus
Golden lilies, snowy white daisies,
Lavender, rosemary, violets blue,
Mary, we're sewing with love and devotion,
Asking a blessing from Jesus and you.

The three Sisters exit with their chairs

Second Reader June fourteenth. Sister Marie-Bernard has again been confined to the infirmary. The tumour on her right knee seems to be worsening, and she appears to be undergoing a severe spiritual eclipse. Reverend Mother Josephine suspects that she is undergoing a form of purification of the soul.

Two Nuns wheel on a statue of the Virgin Mary. They set it in place, genuflect, move up stage, genuflect again, and go off

A time of incomparable stress caused by a feeling of inability to love God sufficiently, with the resultant terror of eternal loss. Sister Marie-Bernard's condition is causing grave concern.

The Lights cross-fade on to the Chapel

SCENE 3

The Chapel. Evening

The acting area is lit with the flickering glow of candlelight. Mother Marie-Therese enters, goes to the statue and kneels in front of it. After a moment Bernadette enters, dragging herself on a crutch. Mother Marie-Therese rises, crosses herself, and starts to leave. Bernadette approaches her hesitantly

Bernadette Mother?
Marie-Therese (*impersonally*) I have not seen you for some time, Sister, I hope you were well treated in the infirmary.

Act II, Scene 3

Bernadette Although I took the vow of poverty, I am sure the poor were never so well treated as I have been.
Marie-Therese (*moving away*) I hope you continue to make progress, my child.
Bernadette Mother!

Mother Marie-Therese stops

Mother, once you asked me to come to you.
Marie-Therese That was many years ago.
Bernadette Do I have permission to speak to you now?
Marie-Therese I have my duties to attend to.
Bernadette I have no-one to turn to, Mother.
Marie-Therese Your confessor?
Bernadette I have already been to him.
Marie-Therese Then why come to me?
Bernadette Because I thought you would understand.
Marie-Therese What is there to understand?
Bernadette I am consumed by doubt. I feel forsaken. There is no longer any response when I pray.
Marie-Therese That happens to us all from time to time.
Bernadette Never so cruelly as now, Reverend Mother. I feel I cannot love the intangible sufficiently, and I have consequently been abandoned.
Marie-Therese Only you can measure the depth of your own love.
Bernadette Oh, I love him—with all my soul, and my heart. I have offered my pain and humiliation in silence, because it was all I had to offer. But it was insufficient.
Marie-Therese (*after a pause*) You have not changed, Sister. You still seek consolation from the virtues you practise.
Bernadette Oh, no, Mother.
Marie-Therese You are still consumed by your own pride.
Bernadette My pride is a cross I have to bear.
Marie-Therese And you have flaunted it.
Bernadette I have tried to carry it hidden in my heart.
Marie-Therese Then you have failed.
Bernadette I have failed, Mother. But not through want of trying. I have been granted so many graces, and made so little use of them.
Marie-Therese You have been granted no more grace than anyone else in this community. You have been deceived into believing that you are a paragon of all the virtues. A long time ago I told you you were on the common road. Until you believe me, you will know no peace.
Bernadette I have always believed you.
Marie-Therese You have set yourself up as someone spiritually privileged.
Bernadette I have only tried to express my gratitude for what happened at Lourdes.
Marie-Therese Sister Marie-Bernard, did it happen?

There is a pause as Bernadette stares at her incredulously

The truth need not leave the walls of this chapel.

Bernadette seems to struggle for words

Bernadette I saw her.
Marie-Therese Disease and poverty play extraordinary tricks on a child's mind, Sister.
Bernadette I saw her!
Marie-Therese But it was not a vision of the Blessed Virgin. Was it? Was it? Do you think that if she had deigned to appear to you, she would abandon you now?

Bernadette stares at her

Bernadette I saw her!
Marie-Therese For a long time I have known the truth. I was reluctant to enlighten you because your belief was a spur to your vocation. But now I feel that your vocation is secure, and the time has come for you to face reality.
Bernadette I have never evaded reality since I saw it in the grotto years ago.
Marie-Therese Is your mind so clouded that you are incapable of accepting the truth?
Bernadette The truth?
Marie-Therese My child! You were hallucinated.
Bernadette The doctors in Lourdes said I was the same as anyone else.
Marie-Therese I am merely confirming the conclusions of a panel of doctors more distinguished than those who examined you at Lourdes.
Bernadette Who are they, Mother?
Marie-Therese The Society of Doctors of Orne.
Bernadette But they have never examined me.
Marie-Therese They studied your case meticulously.
Bernadette And you agree with them?
Marie-Therese These are wise men.
Bernadette I am sane.
Marie-Therese One of the symptoms of insanity is the inability to see it in one's self.
Bernadette But you know me, Mother!
Marie-Therese Oh, I know you! I know a young woman who claims to have seen things no-one else has seen. Someone who debased herself before a multitude by grovelling about on a filthy grotto floor——
Bernadette There was a reason.
Marie-Therese —besmirching her face with mud . . .
Bernadette She told me!
Marie-Therese The distorted mind always finds a reason for the contortions of the body it inhabits.

Bernadette stares at her anxiously

Would the Immaculate Mother reduce her *own* to the slobbering depravity of an animal? Do you honestly believe that heaven would descend to a refuse pit frequented by swine?
Bernadette I am frightened . . .

Act II, Scene 3

Marie-Therese Then I am beginning to reach you at last.
Bernadette (*bewildered*) But she is still in my head, even now, so clear—beautiful. And I can still hear her voice—how can there be any doubt about that?
Marie-Therese Have you ever visited an asylum? I have. Poor lost souls, burnt up in the intensity of their delusions.
Bernadette (*unsure*) I am not like them, Mother.
Marie-Therese You have never shown proof to the contrary.
Bernadette My pain is no delusion.
Marie-Therese Then rid yourself of it.
Bernadette My pain is not self-imposed to be turned on and off at will. My pain is my penance.
Marie-Therese Is it? Sometimes pain is rooted in desire.
Bernadette I have accepted it, but never desired it.
Marie-Therese But you have admitted that as your physical agony intensifies so does your doubt.
Bernadette I no longer know what I say! My knee! The agony blurs my mind . . .
Marie-Therese Then you admit your body has taken precedence over your soul?
Bernadette No, Mother . . .
Marie-Therese You admit that your suffering is greater than your love for her?
Bernadette No, no! Help me, Mother. Help me.
Marie-Therese (*weighing her words*) Sister—permission could be granted for you to return to Lourdes.
Bernadette For what reason? My mission there is ended.
Marie-Therese Ended? If so, then I suggest that your Lady of the Grotto is sadly lacking in compassion.
Bernadette Oh, no . . .
Marie-Therese Is it compassionate to supplant faith with doubt? For that is what she has done. If you were ever granted a mission, then I suggest it is incomplete.
Bernadette If only I could ease your doubts . . .
Marie-Therese You can. Return to Lourdes and offer yourself as final proof. Go and implore her intercession on your behalf.

Bernadette tries to interrupt, but Marie-Therese continues speaking

Pulmonary cases, such as yours, have been cured in the Spring—the lame have been made to walk. If you believe that these cures are through the direct intercession of our Blessed Lady, then offer yourself to be healed. I know that you have repeatedly stressed that the Spring is not for you . . .
Bernadette It isn't.
Marie-Therese But do you honestly believe that she would look on your agony without compassion? Would she choose you, then, having used you, leave you sick and uncertain? Is this your conception of the Holy Mother of God?

Bernadette No.

Marie-Therese Then consider the possibilities of a cure, my child. To walk without pain. To breathe freely. To follow your vocation with diligence, instead of being a liability to us all. (*A pause*) The decision is yours.

Bernadette (*after a long pause*) When may I leave Mother?

Marie-Therese (*moving away*) I shall make arrangements.

Bernadette (*with sudden strength*) No!

Marie-Therese turns back

I cannot go!

There is a pause, as Marie-Therese stares at her

Marie-Therese (*slowly*) So at last I know the truth! At last I have the proof I have been seeking all these years.

Bernadette Proof? What proof?

Marie-Therese The implication is obvious, isn't it? You deny the miraculous source of the Spring!

Bernadette No!

Marie-Therese The world soon forgets, Sister. And with forgetfulness comes forgiveness. Accept the decision of the Doctors of Orne, and renounce what you claim to have seen in the Grotto as the distortion of an unbalanced mind.

Bernadette I renounce nothing!

Marie-Therese stiffens

What I suffer now is only a continuation of my mission at Lourdes, when I promised to do penance, mortify myself, and pray for sinners.

Marie-Therese You are not prepared to take my advice?

Bernadette The price is too great. I can accept the physical suffering. What I cannot accept is the torture of my inner suffering. I cannot live alone in this darkness.

Marie-Therese You are the victim of your own delusion.

Bernadette Then I must live with my delusion, because there is nothing else to take its place.

Marie-Therese And I can no longer help you.

Bernadette Neither you nor any other human person.

Marie-Therese Then enjoy your delusion, Sister Marie-Bernard. I shall continue to pray for you.

Bernadette Pray for my soul, Mother. My body is of no consequence.

Mother Marie-Therese goes off

Oh, compassionate Heart of Jesus, accept my agony as supplication for those that suffer, that weep and forget you. From this moment on, I have severed myself from all hope of human understanding. You have given me the strength to break my will and blend it with yours, now give me

Act II, Scene 3

the will to endure the pain my heart suffers. (*She raises her arms in a penitential sign of the crucifixion. Her crutch clatters to the floor*)

The Nuns enter from the main chapel and slowly surround Bernadette

Oh, Jesus, if you want me crucified, then crucify me. But don't desert me in this my hour of need. Oh, God, have mercy. Holy Mother, pray for me!

Bernadette turns and takes a stumbling step towards the statue of the Blessed Virgin, her face contorted with agony. Then she sighs and collapses in a faint

The Nuns lift her and carry her off, one taking the crutch

The Lights cross-fade on to the Readers. During the following the Nuns clear the Chapel setting, wheeling off the statue, and the Infirmary scene is brought on

LINKING SCENE

First Reader The Community Journal. December eighth. Sister Marie-Bernard's condition continues to give grave cause for anxiety. The tumour on her knee has assumed alarming proportions, and the agony is aggravated by the spread of caries which rage through her bones with the most violent intensity.

Second Reader December eleventh. Sister Marie-Bernard has started to haemorrhage from the lungs. Her suffering is so acute that the entire community exert their prayers in an effort to ease her pain. She is chronically insomniac; spending entire nights without sleeping, and when finally overcome with exhaustion she is awakened by acute pain which tortures her unceasingly.

First Reader December thirteenth. A Commission has arrived from Rome to re-question Sister Marie-Bernard about the apparitions. She solemnly reaffirmed what she had stated as a child. When cross-examined about the most minute and exacting details, Sister Marie-Bernard finally objected from sheer exhaustion.

Two Nuns bring on the bed, with Bernadette in it. Another brings in a chair Sister Marthe Fores enters with a stool and sets it in front of the chair. She then sits on the chair, takes out a small missal and reads it

The good fathers apologized with grace, explaining that they did not realize the extent of her debility.

Second Reader January seventh, eighteen hundred and seventy-nine. Sister Marie-Bernard is thirty-five years old today.

The Lights cross-fade to the Infirmary

Scene 4

The Infirmary

Bernadette is propped up in bed. Sister Marthe Fores sits in a chair reading her missal. Bernadette writhes from side to side. Her face is bathed in sweat. She stifles a moan from time to time, then starts coughing. Sister Marthe Fores rushes to her side

Marthe Fores Sister Marie-Bernard . . . (*She goes and pulls a bell-rope*)

A bell is heard ringing off

The doctor will be here soon.

Bernadette makes an effort to speak, but no sound comes

Rest, Sister. Don't try to speak.

The Doctor comes hurrying in

Quickly, Doctor. The congestion is intensifying.

The Doctor takes Bernadette's pulse

Doctor I want you to sit up, Sister.

Bernadette weakly shakes her head

It will help you to breathe more easily.

Bernadette struggles desperately, but sinks back exhausted

(*To Sister Marthe Fores*) Sister, you will have to help me carry her to the chair.
Marthe-Fores That is impossible, Doctor.
Doctor But necessary.
Marthe-Fores Her bones are brittle, and her nerves so inflamed she cannot bear the weight of a sheet.
Doctor I am aware of that, Sister. But unless we move her immediately she will choke to death. Please call for assistance.

Sister Marthe Fores pulls the bell-rope. The Doctor wipes Bernadette's brow

There, Sister. You will soon be more comfortable. (*Pointing to the stool*) Sister, the stool.
Bernadette (*gasping*) Oh, my God—my God . . .
Doctor Don't talk.

Sister Emilienne hurries in

Quickly, Sisters. You must each support a leg. I must stress the agony the patient is undergoing, so I beseech you to exercise your utmost gentleness and skill.

Sister Marthe Fores and Emilienne each grasp a leg. The Doctor supports Bernadette under the arms. She gives a low suppressed moan. The Doctor nods, and they carry her to the chair. She writhes, and her mouth opens in a suppressed scream. Then she faints. Visually one is reminded of a Pieta as they lay the unconscious Nun on a chair, her leg supported by a footstool. They revive her by chaffing her wrists and holding a smelling bottle to her nose. Sister Marthe Fores holds a glass of water to her lips. Bernadette revives weakly

The end is here. Please summon the Mother-General.

Sister Emilienne leaves. Sister Vincent Garros enters—she seeks permission from the Doctor to approach the patient

Sister Vincent Garros goes to Bernadette, who gently inclines her head and smiles. Sister Vincent Garros takes her hand

Vincent Garros Sister Marie-Bernard?
Bernadette (*weakly*) Good-bye, Vincent—this time it really is over. Do not weep . . . (*She withdraws her hand*)
Vincent Garros (*gently*) I do not weep, Sister. I remember the promise. "I cannot make you happy in this world——
Bernadette —but in the next . . ."
Vincent Garros The beginning will be soon, Sister.

Sister Emilienne returns with Mother Josephine and Father Douce. They are followed by as many Nuns as available. As their backs will be towards the audience and they are in shadow, their indentities are unimportant. The Nuns kneel silently in prayer

Josephine My child . . .

Bernadette smiles at her, then slowly looks at each of the Nuns

Bernadette Mother Marie-Therese?
Josephine She is unwell, Sister, and unable to be with you.
Bernadette Tell her—I saw her . . .
Josephine Do you have a last request?
Bernadette Forgiveness . . .
Josephine There is nothing to forgive, my daughter.
Bernadette Forgiveness—for the trouble I have caused. I hadn't the strength of soul—to follow the religious life—faithfully . . .
Josephine We are well satisfied, Sister.
Bernadette And from the sisters—I ask forgiveness for the bad example I have shown them. (*Her voice a shade firmer*) And above all, I beg forgiveness for my—pride . . .

Bernadette agonizingly extends her arms in the sign of crucifixion

Doctor Conserve your energy, Sister.

Bernadette Reverend Mother, pray for me, pray for me . . .

Josephine I shall ask the Immaculate Mother to console your suffering.

Bernadette (*shaking her head*) No consolation. Ask for patience and strength. The agony is good for—the soul. (*Her voice is filled with yearning*) I saw her. I saw her . . . (*Suddenly she looks into blackness with surprise. An expression of extreme ecstacy overcomes her. She seems to radiate an inner glow. With hands clutching the arms of the chair she attempts to raise herself. She reaches out into space with both arms, and gives a long sigh. She makes a majestic sign of the cross and sinks back*)

Father Douce puts a crucifix in Bernadette's hands. She closes her eyes

Josephine (*quietly*) Hail Mary, full of grace. The Lord is with thee. Blessed art thou among women, and blessed is the fruit of thy womb, Jesus.

At this point of the prayer Bernadette joins in, her voice firm but gradually fading away. Mother Josephine stops

Bernadette Holy Mary, Mother of God, pray for me—poor sinner—poor sinner . . . (*She gives a gentle sigh and slumps into total relaxation*)

The Doctor checks Bernadette's pulse and shakes his head at an enquiring look from Mother Josephine. He closes Bernadette's eyes. Father Douce approaches and gives Bernadette his blessing

Mother Josephine kisses Bernadette's forehead, then goes out

The Nuns all rise and start to form a group around the chair as the Lights cross-fade on to the Readers

LINKING SCENE

During the reading, the Doctor and Father Douce wheel Bernadette's bed off, the Nuns remove the Infirmary furniture, and the scene is set for Mother Marie-Therese's cell

A bell tolls

First Reader April seventeenth. Despite the heavy rain, thousands of people have come from all over the country for the "lying-in-state" of Sister Marie-Bernard.

Second Reader The throngs became so great that the Police Commissioner had to be summoned to exercise his authority in controlling them.

First Reader Ascension Day. May twenty-second. Sister Marie-Bernard was buried today in the chapel of St Joseph, in the Convent of St Gildard, in Nevers.

Very softly, the Lourdes Hymn sung by the pilgrims in procession steals in. It continues under the following, increasing in volume into the next scene

Act II, Scene 5

Second Reader Community Journal. July eleventh, nineteen hundred and six. Mother Marie-Therese Vauzou, a former Mistress of Novices, today celebrates her diamond jubilee in the religious profession. Although retired to the Convent of Mary Immaculate in Lourdes, Mother Marie-Therese is strongly in our thoughts.
First Reader We offer her our congratulations on this wonderful day, and join in her great happiness.
Second Reader How we wish we could all be with her in Lourdes.

The Lights cross-fade on to the main set

Scene 5

A cell in the Convent of Mary Immaculate of Lourdes

The cell is sparsely furnished—a bed, a chair, a table. A crucifix is the sole adornment on the stark walls. There is an open window through which can be seen the grotto and the basilica rising above it

There is a crescendo of sound; all the bells in Lourdes appear to be ringing, the invocations at the grotto clash with the Lourdes Hymn being sung by a passing procession

Mother Marie-Therese enters. She is now over eighty, but still maintains a rigid discipline of body. It is obvious from her expression that the sound causes her almost real physical discomfort. She moves to the window and slams the shutters. Immediately all sound ceases. Sister Paschal hurries in

Paschal Mother Marie-Therese, are you all right?

Mother Marie-Therese glowers at her

You left the celebration so hurriedly . . .
Marie-Therese Those people . . .
Paschal They have come to honour you.
Marie-Therese They have come to stare at me. I will not tolerate their curiosity. (*She picks up a book from her bed*)
Paschal You interest them, Mother.
Marie-Therese For the wrong reason.
Paschal It is customary to celebrate a jubilee in the religious life.
Marie-Therese I do not approve of wasted time.
Paschal Your life has not been wasted, Mother.
Marie-Therese Who are you to judge?
Paschal You are not being judged.
Marie-Therese I have been judged and condemned. (*She sits on the chair and reads*)
Paschal No, you are mistaken.
Marie-Therese If I have not been condemned then why have I been sent here? Why have I been sent to Lourdes of all places?

Paschal We consider it a privilege to be retired to Lourdes. (*She moves towards the shuttered window*)
Marie-Therese What are you doing?
Paschal Letting in some fresh air.
Marie-Therese Leave that window alone!
Paschal Forgive me, Sister. I meant no harm.

Sister Paschal moves towards the door

Marie-Therese Don't leave me. I who cherished my privacy can no longer bear solitude. I am tormented by mental anguish, and my loneliness only intensifies it.

There is a tap at the door. Sister Louise enters

Louise I have been asked to summon you, Mother Marie-Therese.
Marie-Therese I am in retirement, and no longer subject to anyone.
Louise But you are missed, Mother. It is your diamond jubilee and you are not celebrating.
Paschal Please tell Reverend Mother that Mother Marie-Therese is tired and begs to be excused.
Louise But there are so many dignitaries waiting to meet her.
Marie-Therese I am old and weary. Why must I be subjected to a tirade of questions about that girl? She is the only reason my company is desired nowadays.
Paschal You know that isn't true.
Louise The Bishop of Nevers is asking for you.
Paschal Bishop Forcade?
Louise He is awaiting you, Mother.
Marie-Therese Must I face him in front of others?
Paschal Permission might be granted for you to meet him here. It would be a kindness to see an old man. Won't you meet him, Mother?
Marie-Therese (*after a pause*) Would you be so kind as to ask Reverend Mother if this would be possible?

Louise leaves

Paschal He is a fine man. Only surpassed in the guidance of souls by yourself, Mother.
Marie-Therese Don't try to humour me!
Paschal I am not trying to humour you.
Marie-Therese Then you pander to my age.
Paschal Your judgement has guided so many vocations.
Marie-Therese With one soul I received no light to guide me. God gave her to me without help or hindrance. He offered me entire responsibility. I failed. (*She retreats into her memory.*) From the moment I saw her I lost all peace of mind. The mere sight of the girl antagonized my heart.
Paschal That was a long time ago.

Act II, Scene 5   51

Marie-Therese I could not address her unless I did so bitingly.
Paschal (*soothing*) Mother...
Marie-Therese And now they are clamouring to have her sanctified. They will be cruelly disillusioned by their failure.

Sister Paschal checks a reaction

Marie-Therese What is it?
Paschal Nothing.
Marie-Therese Something is disturbing you.
Paschal No.
Marie-Therese Do you know something that has been kept from me? What?
Paschal Mother Forestier has just returned from Rome. The cause of Bernadette's canonization is to be introduced.

There is a long pause

Marie-Therese Then tell them to wait until I am dead.

Another pause

For I shall not speak up for her.

A longer pause

If necessary I shall turn Devil's Advocate in the Cause of Canonization!
Paschal (*a shocked gasp*) Mother!
Marie-Therese I am the only one who really knew her.

There is a knock at the door. Sister Paschal admits the Bishop of Nevers, now an old man in his eighties

Paschal Mother?

Sister Marie-Therese sits stiffly, staring unblinkingly into space, neither seeing nor caring

Mother Marie-Therese! His Lordship.
Bishop It has been a long time, Mother.

Mother Marie-Therese stares at him for a moment

Marie-Therese Your presence is no longer required, Sister Paschal.

Sister Paschal quietly leaves

Marie-Therese pulls herself heavily from her chair. She tries to kiss the Bishop's ring, but he stops her by helping her up

Bishop I have come to offer congratulations.
Marie-Therese To an old woman riddled with spiritual doubt?
Bishop (*with humour*) I was given to believe that you prided yourself on your faith.

Marie-Therese All the more reason to despise one's pride.
Bishop Pride is merely a retention of the natural character.
Marie-Therese I have suffered to eliminate all traces of the natural character.
Bishop And therein lies your weakness. You expect too much of the self.
Marie-Therese When one demands perfection an example must be set.
Bishop And what example do you set by your isolation?
Marie-Therese God has put me under detention, my Lord, in the one place I hoped never to be.
Bishop You are here only in the hope that some of the joy of Lourdes will be assimilated by your soul.
Marie-Therese The place sickens me.
Bishop Why?
Marie-Therese Its crass commercialism reeks of the devil.
Bishop It has been ordained a holy place.
Marie-Therese It is a market-place for vulgarity.
Bishop Would you deny the pilgrims a memento of their visit? Don't forget that their happiness is as deep-rooted as your aversion.
Marie-Therese Their happiness wil be short lived when her cause is dismissed.
Bishop You are convinced that it will be?
Marie-Therese The Blessed Virgin did not appear to her.
Bishop Whether she did or not is superfluous to the subject.
Marie-Therese The subject, surely, is the introduction of her cause?
Bishop And you are as aware as I am that nobody was ever canonized on the grounds of supernatural apparitions. If she is canonized, it will be for the high level of Christian integrity with which she conducted her life.
Marie-Therese She was not without fault.
Bishop If she were, she would have had nothing to overcome.
Marie-Therese (*after a pause*) You have come here to condemn me.
Bishop No.
Marie-Therese You have heard of my treatment toward her and now you have come to condemn me like all the others!
Bishop No. (*A pause*) Mother Marie-Therese . . .
Marie-Therese Continue, my Lord, I am not one to avoid retribution.
Bishop Do you believe your behaviour toward her was justified?
Marie-Therese I was—incapable of behaving in any other way.
Bishop But was it justified?
Marie-Therese It caused me remorse.
Bishop Yet you did nothing to alleviate your remorse?
Marie-Therese I was incapable . . .
Bishop Were you incapable of easing her suffering?
Marie-Therese (*with an anguished cry*) Don't probe my wounds!
Bishop Why?
Marie-Therese My tongue could not express what was in my heart. To address her was to wound her.

Bishop You are a Sister of Charity, devout, pious and kind. Why then were you incapable of easing a fellow human being's suffering?
Marie-Therese I alone disbelieved her!
Bishop (*after a pause*) Sister Marie-Therese, stop blaming yourself. Your lack of belief was not of your making.
Marie-Therese And now you patronize me, too?
Bishop I am an old man with neither the cause nor the patience to patronize an old woman.
Marie-Therese Then why try to exonerate my treatment of the girl?
Bishop If you had lightened the girl's burden—if you had been capable of giving her the merest grain of happiness, how could the Blessed Virgin's prediction have been fulfilled?
Marie-Therese (*after a pause*) I don't understand you.
Bishop "I cannot make you happy in this world, but I promise to do so in the next."

Sister Marie-Therese stares at him

Should the Congregation of Rights affirm Bernadette Soubirous's cause, you will be recognized as the integral contributor to her glorification
Marie-Therese (*scandalized*) I?
Bishop You.
Marie-Therese You say that I was the principal object she had to overcome.
Bishop Can't you understand?
Marie-Therese No!
Bishop (*irritated*) Try!
Marie-Therese I understand nothing.
Bishop (*impatiently*) Then accept your consolation without understanding.
Marie-Therese I am not here for consolation.

The Bishop opens the window. The cell is gently flooded with the softly murmured Litany of Our Lady

Bishop Look.
Marie-Therese No.
Bishop (*losing patience*) Look!
Marie-Therese (*stubbornly turning her head away*) I do not acquiesce in superstition.
Bishop What do you fear?

Mother Marie-Therese gives a disdainful toss of her head

If you have nothing to fear, then I challenge you to look!

Mother Marie-Therese slowly walks towards the window. She looks out then turns her back on the view

Marie-Therese Such deception is cruel. Only a minority will be cured.
Bishop The majority will receive a special grace. The grace to suffer well. An example was chosen. Bernadette fulfilled her mission. And you, Mother, were an instrument in the fulfilment. (*He looks out of the win-*

dow. Conversationally) The Blessed Virgin showed good taste in choosing this place. The mountains—such tranquillity—such peace. (*He turns to Mother Marie-Therese*) Good-bye, Mother Marie-Therese. God bless you.

The Bishop leaves

Marie-Therese (*uttering a deep shattering prayer of anguish*) Oh, God—I believe. I believe. Help thou my unbelief. (*She painfully bends and kisses the floor in penance*)

The Lights remain on her, but come up on the two Readers

First Reader On February fifteenth, nineteen hundred and seven, Mother Marie-Therese Vauzou died in her eighty-second year after imploring the intercession of Our Lady of Lourdes.
Second Reader On December eighth, nineteen-thirty-three. The Feast of the Immaculate Conception. Sister Marie-Bernard was canonized and will be known henceforth as Saint Bernadette.

The canonization bells start to peal triumphantly. Mother Marie-Therese slowly raises her arms in acceptance, as—

the CURTAIN *falls*

FURNITURE AND PROPERTY LIST

NOTE: All furniture, except the two lecterns for the Readers, is taken on and off during the action by members of the cast as indicated. The following list is therefore divided into Furniture and Properties.

ACT I

FURNITURE

OFFICE (Scenes 1 and 3)
        Table or desk. *On it:* writing materials
        Armchair
        2 small chairs

GREAT HALL (Scenes 2 and 5)
        Rostrum with steps and lectern
        (Scene 5) Bishop's chair

BERNADETTE'S ROOM IN THE INFIRMARY (Scene 4)
        Small iron bed, armchair

PROPERTIES

On stage: *On desk:* handbell, letter

Off stage: Folded veil, crucifix, rosary, manual, Rule Book **(Vincent Garros)**
        Medical bag with stethoscope and instruments **(Doctor)**
        Bunches of white flowers **(Nuns)**
        Black nun's veil **(Josephine)**
        4 Letters of Appointment **(Bishop)**
        4 Rule Books **(Josephine)**
        Travelling bag, umbrella **(Paschal)**

Personal: **Bishop:** ring

ACT II

FURNITURE

INFIRMARY (Scene 1)
        2 small iron beds
        Medicine cabinet

OFFICE (Scene 2)
        As Act I, Scene 1

CHAPEL (Scene 3)
    Statue of Virgin Mary

BERNADETTE'S ROOM IN THE INFIRMARY (Scene 4)
    Small iron bed
    Small chair
    Stool
    Bell-rope

MARIE-THERESE'S CELL (Scene 5)
    Small bed
    Table
    2 small chairs
    Chest
    On wall: Crucifix

PROPERTIES

On stage: On bed in Scene 5: book

Off stage: Pail and scrubbing brush (**Bernadette**)
    Blankets (**Marthe Fores, Nun**)
    School books (**Paschal**)
    Sheets (**Vincent Garros, Emilienne**)
    Missal (**Josephine**)
    3 chairs (**Bernadette, Vincent Garros, Emilienne**)
    Sewing materials (**Bernadette, Vincent Garros, Emilienne**)
    Crutch (**Bernadette**)
    Missal (**Marthe Fores**)
    Smelling bottle, glass of water (**Nuns**)
    Crucifix (**Fathes Douce**)

Personal: **Josephine:** walking-stick

GROUND PLANS

Area of false stage used in the original production is indicated by dotted lines.

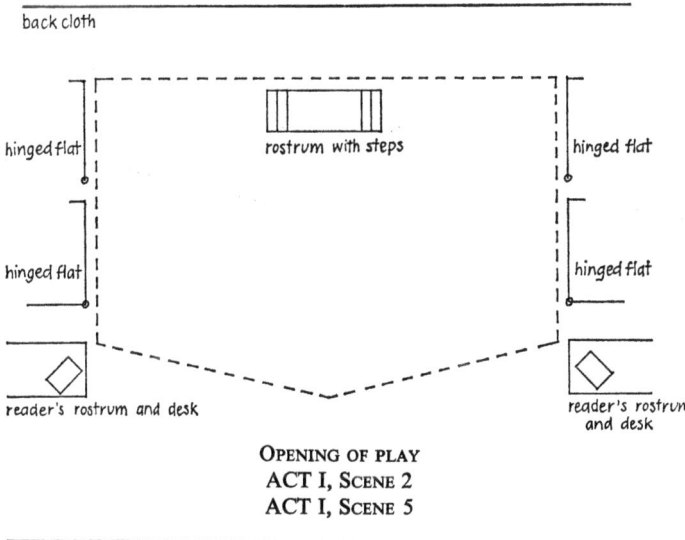

OPENING OF PLAY
ACT I, SCENE 2
ACT I, SCENE 5

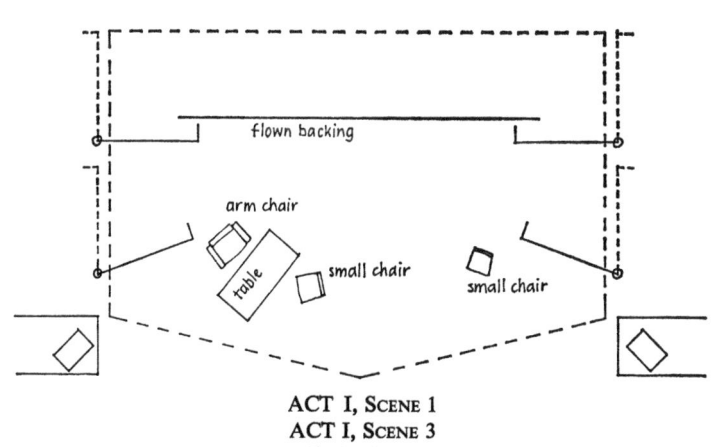

ACT I, SCENE 1
ACT I, SCENE 3
ACT II, SCENE 2

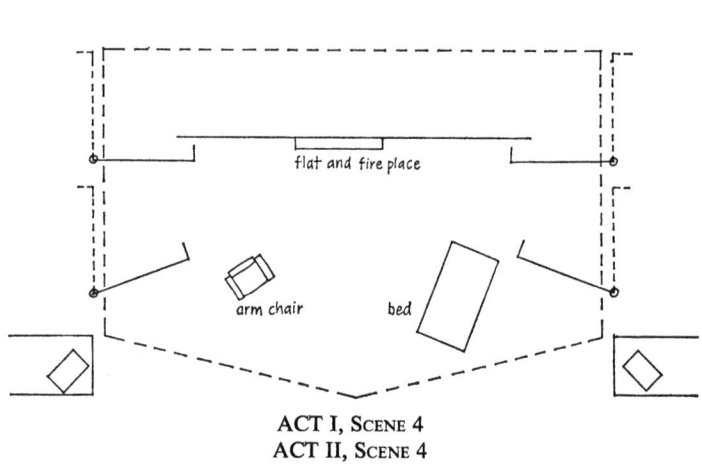

ACT I, Scene 4
ACT II, Scene 4

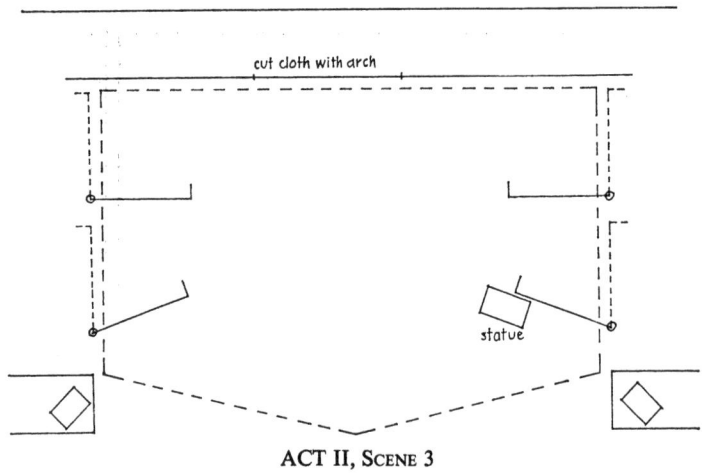

ACT II, Scene 3

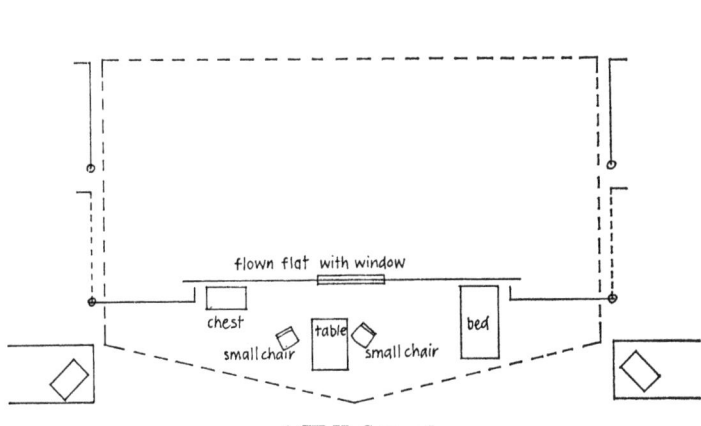

ACT II, SCENE 5

LIGHTING PLOT

Property fittings required: nil
Standing set

ACT I

To open:	Spots on Readers, R and L	
Cue 1	**Josephine** signs letter	(Page 1)
	General lighting full up—day	
Cue 2	**Bishop** and **Josephine** exit	(Page 6)
	Cross-fade to Readers	
Cue 3	**First Reader:** ". . . and retiring nature."	(Page 6)
	Cross-fade to general lighting—day	
Cue 4	**Marie-Therese:** "Do you understand?"	(Page 14)
	Cross-fade to Readers	
Cue 5	**Second Reader:** ". . . of Extreme Unction."	(Page 14)
	Cross-fade to general lighting—night	
Cue 6	**Josephine:** "Please follow me."	(Page 18)
	Fade to semi-Black-Out	
Cue 7	When scene change completed	(Page 18)
	Fade up to general lighting—night	
Cue 8	**Bernadette:** "Strike the hammer gently, Mother."	(Page 21)
	Cross-fade to Readers	
Cue 9	**Second Reader:** ". . . withheld from her."	(Page 21)
	Cross-fade to general lighting—day	

ACT II

To open:	Spots on Readers, R and L	
Cue 10	**Second Reader:** ". . . the more serious cases."	(Page 28)
	Cross-fade to shadowy pool of light C—night	
Cue 11	**Marie-Therese** exits	(Page 34)
	Fade to semi-Black-Out	
Cue 12	When scene change complete	(Page 34)
	Fade up to general lighting—day	
Cue 13	**Doctor** exits	(Page 39)
	Cross-fade to Readers	
Cue 14	**Second Reader:** ". . . causing grave concern."	(Page 40)
	Cross-fade to general lighting—candle-light effect—evening	
Cue 15	**Nuns** carry **Bernadette** off	(Page 45)
	Cross-fade to Speakers	
Cue 16	**Second Reader:** ". . . years old today."	(Page 45)
	Cross-fade to general lighting—evening	
Cue 17	**Nuns** form group round **Bernadette**	(Page 48)
	Cross-fade to Readers	
Cue 18	**Second Reader:** ". . . with her in Lourdes."	(Page 49)
	Cross-fade to general lighting—evening	
Cue 19	**Marie-Therese** kisses floor	(Page 54)
	Spots up on Readers, retain general lighting	

EFFECTS PLOT

ACT I

Cue 1	**Sister Marthe Fores** exits *Gentle murmur of Nun's voices, continue for a few moments*	(Page 8)
Cue 2	**Bernadette:** "I am the Immaculate Conception." *The Angelus rings*	(Page 11)
Cue 3	**Josephine:** "Please follow me." *Litany of Our Lady is heard—continue until scene change complete*	(Page 18)

ACT II

Cue 4	**Marthe Fores:** ". . . making her rounds soon!" *Bell rings*	(Page 29)
Cue 5	**Marie-Therese** leaves angrily *The Office is heard being sung—continue until scene change complete*	(Page 34)
Cue 6	**Marthe Fores** pulls bell-rope *Bell rings*	(Page 46)
Cue 7	**Marthe Fores** pulls bell-rope *Bell rings*	(Page 46)
Cue 8	Nuns wheel **Bernadette** off *Bell tolls*	(Page 48)
Cue 9	**First Reader:** ". . . St Gildard, in Nevers." *Bell fades as Lourdes Hymn starts very softly sung, gradually rising through Linking Scene and opening of scene following*	(Page 48)
Cue 10	Scene 5 opens *Add sound of bells and invocations to Lourdes Hymn, crescendo*	(Page 49)
Cue 11	**Marie-Therese** shuts window *Cut all sound*	(Page 49)
Cue 12	**Second Reader:** ". . . as Saint Bernadette." *Canonization bells peal—continue to Curtain*	(Page 54)

Although John Kerr was born in Rhodesia, he has lived in England for over twenty years. For a short period he was an actor and appeared in repertory and films. He has travelled extensively and it was while he was visiting Lourdes three years ago that his interest was first aroused in Bernadette and inspired the play *Mistress of Novices*. This is his second West End play—the first being *On a Foggy Day* which starred Margaret Lockwood and Siobhan McKenna. A third play of his, *Memory of Another Summer*, was performed at the Connaught Theatre, Worthing.

The play *Mistress of Novices* recounts the story of Bernadette and the miraculous vision she claims to have been granted, and also the conflict that this assertion causes in her relationship with the sceptical and strong-willed Mother of Novices. Set mainly in the convent of St Gildard, Nevers, it follows the life of Bernadette until its agonized end, moves to Lourdes for a final scene when the Mistress of Novices is an aged woman and closes with the announcement of Bernadette's canonization. The action can be set against tabs and wings with the simplest of furnishings. Period: mid-nineteenth century to early twentieth century.

ISBN 0 573 06012 6

www.ingramcontent.com/pod-product-compliance
Ingram Content Group UK Ltd.
Pitfield, Milton Keynes, MK11 3LW, UK
UKHW021846210426
5322IPUK00022B/507